ISBN 978-1-331-69309-3
PIBN 10222326

# 1 MONTH OF
# FREE
# READING

at

## www.ForgottenBooks.com

By purchasing this book you are
eligible for one month membership to
ForgottenBooks.com, giving you
unlimited access to our entire
collection of over 700,000 titles via
our web site and mobile apps.

To claim your free month visit:

www.forgottenbooks.com/free222326

English
Français
Deutsche
Italiano
Español
Português

# www.forgottenbooks.com

**Mythology** Photography **Fiction**
Fishing Christianity **Art** Cooking
Essays Buddhism Freemasonry
Medicine **Biology** Music **Ancient
Egypt** Evolution Carpentry Physics
Dance Geology **Mathematics** Fitness
Shakespeare **Folklore** Yoga Marketing
**Confidence** Immortality Biographies
Poetry **Psychology** Witchcraft
Electronics Chemistry History **Law**
Accounting **Philosophy** Anthropology
Alchemy Drama Quantum Mechanics
Atheism Sexual Health **Ancient History**
**Entrepreneurship** Languages Sport
Paleontology Needlework Islam
**Metaphysics** Investment Archaeology
Parenting Statistics Criminology
**Motivational**

# *Acknowledgments*

Grateful acknowledgment is made to the following:

To the Bodleian Library, Oxford, to the British Museum, London, to the Lambeth Palace Library, and to Cambridge University Library for information and copies of original manuscripts.

To the American Historical Society, New York, to the Folger Library, Washington, and to Yale University Library for the use of source materials.

To the library of Union Theological Seminary, New York, and to the rare book room of the New York Public Library, for valuable aid in research.

To Miss Margaret T. Hills of the American Bible Society, New York, for the loan of illustrative prints.

To the National Portrait Gallery, London, for the portrait of Bishop Bancroft.

To Dr. Frederick C. Grant of Union Theological Seminary for comment on the Bois notes.

To the Public Trustee for the Estate of Bernard Shaw, and to the Society of Authors, London, for permission to quote from the preface to *Adventures of the Black Girl in Her Search for God.*

And to Wanda Willson Whitman, the friend who has been associated with this book from the very start. It was she who suggested the original idea, nourished it with her interest and encouragement, and, when the author was no longer here to complete his work, edited the manuscript with skill, integrity, and affection.

# Preface

What good can it do us to know more about the men who made the King James Bible and about their work on it? Just how did these chosen men revise the Bible from 1604 to 1611? Who were these men and what were their careers? Were they happy in their labor? Did they live with success after they finished it? How did it affect them? How does the King James Bible differ from Bibles before and after it? Could a group or groups turn out better writing than a single person? These are some of the questions I aim to answer in this volume.

The King James men were minor writers, though great scholars, doing superb writing. Their task lifted them above themselves, while they leaned firmly on their subjects. Many have written in wonder about what they achieved. I quote here only from one ardent man with Bible learning, and from one who admired the product while he scorned ways of worship.

Dr. F. William Faber: "It lives on the ear like a music that can never be forgotten, like the sound of church bells, which the convert hardly knows how he can forego. Its felicities often seem to be almost things rather than mere words. It is part of the national mind and the anchor of national seriousness. The memory of the dead passes into it. The potent traditions of childhood are stereotyped in its verses. The power of all the griefs and trials of a man is hidden beneath its words. It is the representative of his best moments; and all that there has been about him of soft, and gentle, and pure, and penitent, and good speaks to him for ever out of his English Bible."

H. L. Mencken: "It is the most beautiful of all the translations of the Bible; indeed, it is probably the most beautiful piece of writing in all the literature of the world. Many attempts have been made to purge it of its errors and obscurities. An English Revised Version was published in 1885 and an American Revised Version in 1901, and since then many learned but misguided men have sought to produce translations that should be mathematically accurate, and in the plain speech of everyday. But the Authorized Version has never yielded to any of them, for it is palpably and overwhelmingly better than they are, just as it is better than the Greek New Testament, or the Vulgate, or the Septuagint. Its English is extraordinarily simple, pure, eloquent, and lovely. It is a mine of lordly and incomparable poetry, at once the most stirring and the most touching ever heard of."

One of its great virtues is that it allows and impels us to put any part of it into other words, into our words, that we may get glimpses of more meanings from it and then turn back to it with more delight and profit than ever before. The King James men surpassed us in these respects, that they were scholars, and that they had Elizabethan command over language. At the same time they were like us, of the people, earnest, and at the bottom sweet and sound. We surpass them in our wide modern range of words. At present many urge us in all sorts of projects to "do it yourself." I hope that as you read about these men and what they did you may feel the urge to create the Bible afresh for yourself, to revise the phrases in any way you please, and then to compare your wordings with what we have so long deemed our standard Scriptures.

Thus you may keep the Bible alive for yourself, really be active as you read and study it, and be at one with the learned men, those common people who gave us their splendid best.

# Contents

# CHAPTER 1

# At Hampton Court

"May your Majesty be pleased," said Dr. John Rainolds in his address to the king, "to direct that the Bible be now translated, such versions as are extant not answering to the original."

Rainolds was a Puritan, and the Bishop of London felt it his duty to disagree. "If every man's humor might be followed," snorted His Grace, "there would be no end to translating."

King James was quick to put both factions down. "I profess," he said, "I could never yet see a Bible well translated in English, but I think that of Geneva is the worst."

These few dissident words started the greatest writing project the world has ever known, and the greatest achievement of the reign of James I—the making of the English Bible which has ever since borne his name. The day was Monday, January 16, 1604. The scene was the palace at Hampton Court, with its thousand rooms built by Cardinal Wolsey and successfully coveted by Henry VIII.

King James was new to the English throne but his reign in Scotland had already brought him experience of religious differences. Those more than political considerations divided the people who thronged the roads and cheered the new king on his way from Edinburgh to

London. Most urgent of the many pleas received during the royal progress was the Millenary Petition of the Puritans, called so because it had a thousand signers, a tenth of the English clergy. "The fantastical giddy-headed Puritans," wrote the Archbishop of York to the Bishop of Durham, "are very eager that they may be heard."

Another religious faction, the English Roman Catholics, had sent from France a petition for more freedom. The king could overlook the Catholics, but the Puritans had been gaining ground for a generation and their demands were specific. They opposed Sabbathbreaking and the keeping of other holy days, baptism by women in their homes, display of the cross in baptism, bowing at the name Jesus, and other practices considered high church or popish.

James's answer was to call a meeting to talk about what was "pretended to be amiss" in the churches. Because the plague was making havoc in London, where it was to kill thirty thousand, the meeting was first postponed and then set for Hampton Court, a safe distance from the plague-ridden city.

In the huge rose-red brick palace hard by Hounslow Heath, with its stone gargoyles, twisted chimneys, mullioned windows, and cloistered walks, the king and his friends had reveled since before Christmas. For more guests than the thousand rooms could hold, tents stood in the superb gardens and the broad deer park. In December it was too cold and foggy to enjoy the tennis courts, the tilting ground, the bowling alleys beside the swift, chilly Thames. Even James, reared in the cold of Scotland, wore so many clothes that his weak legs could hardly bear the burden. But there was hunting with bows and arrows to warm the blood, and there was sport enough indoors, what with dancing, drinking, and heavy meals cooked in the long brick ovens.

Fireplace heat was a comfort to those near it. Those

away from it endured what the English called a frowst, of about sixty degrees. The air must have been heavy and stale for there is no record of baths in the palace, though the court used perfumes and pomanders and the king kept his hands soft as sarcenet by never washing them, merely dipping the royal fingers into bowls of attar and other balms.

For the entertainment of the court, Shakespeare's actors performed plays for a fee of twenty gold nobles for each day or night, with an extra tip of five marks from the king. After Christmas, in a masque called "The Twelve Goddesses" staged by Inigo Jones, Queen Anne and eleven maids of honor took part. They wore their hair down and many thought their gauze costumes scandalously sheer, although the queen wore over hers a blue mantle embroidered in silver with the weapons and engines of war. Flutes and viols played sweetly. Francis Bacon was present at this performance. The gay season, as brilliant as any in Elizabeth's reign, immediately preceded the parley about church matters.

Instead of asking the Puritans to send men of their own choice, James and his advisers named just four, among them John Rainolds, whom we may justifiably call the father of the King James Bible. President of Corpus Christi College at Oxford, Rainolds was called the most learned man in England. With him to Hampton Court went Laurence Chaderton from Cambridge, who with Rainolds was to become a translator of the new Bible, and two other Puritans who were to have no part in it. The four were not admitted to the meeting until its second day. Confronting them were a group of fifty or sixty high churchmen, the lords of the council, deans, bishops, and even the Archbishop of Canterbury, rich old John Whitgift, though he was not far from death.

The place of meeting was the king's privy chamber, a large room in Henry VIII's state suite on the east side of the clock court.[1] The chief speakers were Richard Bancroft, Bishop of London, Rainolds, and the king.

James, at thirty-seven an old young man who sputtered because his tongue was too large for his mouth, came in and said a few kind words to the lords, and sat down in his chair which was somewhat removed from the cloth of state. Prince Henry, ten years old, sat near his father on a stool. The king took off his hat when he thanked Almighty God for bringing him into the promised land where religion was purely professed.

When Rainolds' turn came, some said that he spoke offhand of the new Bible, amid much talk of other matters. He stressed four points: that the doctrine of the Church might be preserved in purity according to God's word; that good pastors might be planted in all churches to preach the same; that the church government might be sincerely ministered according to God's word; that the Book of Common Prayer might be suited to more increase of piety.

Though these points were hardly disputable, the meeting got into odd wrangles over lesser concerns. The Puritans, though not so much Rainolds, opposed wedding rings. James, who spoke of his queen as "our dearest bedfellow," said, "I was married with a ring and think others scarcely well married without it." James had a good time with jokes; when Rainolds, unmarried, questioned the phrase in the marriage service "with my body I thee worship," the king said, "Many a man speaks of Robin Hood who never shot his bow; if you had a good wife yourself, you would think that all the honor and worship you could do to her would be well bestowed." Rainolds won his laugh later when, in the argument against

[1] As George II altered this part of the palace, no one can now see the spot where Rainolds stood when he proposed the translation. The best account of that day was written by William Barlow, Dean of Chester, who also was to become a translator.

Romish customs, he said, "The Bishop of Rome hath no authority in this land."

Though all tittered at this remark, the king himself, like Rainolds and many others present, had been born in the Church of Rome; the faith the king defended was less than a century old. For all his solemn and flippant talk, James had really but one devout belief—in kingcraft. Though Sir Edward Coke heard him say at the trial of Sir Walter Raleigh, "I will lose the crown and my life before I will alter religion," the crown was his reason for being, and he had experienced enough extremes of religion to know there could be no easy definition of it. In Scotland he had turned from Romanism despite the fact that—or perhaps because—his mother was a Catholic. But in his homeland he had also known too much of Presbyterianism and rabid Calvinism. Perhaps he meant it when he said stoutly enough, "I will never allow in my conscience that the blood of any man shall be shed for diversity of opinions in religion." But he did allow such bloodshed, in an era still bloodstained. After all, James was the son of Mary of Scotland, who helped bring about the death of his father, and he owed his throne to Queen Elizabeth, who had given the word to behead his mother.

To make up for that tragic past he had now to maintain his own divine right as king, sitting among men who, though they knelt to him—Bancroft kept falling to his knees, and even old Archbishop Whitgift knelt—argued among themselves over matters about which he knew and cared little. As the day wore on, more and more points of difference came up.

John Rainolds impugned the policies of Bishop Bancroft and urged that "old, curious, deep and intricate questions might be avoided in the fundamental instruction of a people." Oddly, in view of his own historic position, one of Rainolds' complaints was about the role

[5]

of books. He was against freedom of the press because youthful minds must be protected. "Unlawful and seditious books might be suppressed, at least retained and imparted to a few, for by the liberty of publishing such books so commonly, many young scholars and unsettled minds in both universities and through the whole realm were corrupted and perverted." Why should anyone read what is clearly wrong? Rainolds was for an elite to tussle with the hard sayings while the masses stayed calm, humble, almost dormant. Here the king was nearer modern thought and told Rainolds that, in taxing the Bishop of London that he suffered bad books, he was a better college man than statesman.

Bancroft for his side denounced the Puritans to his Majesty as "Cartwright's scholars"—their leader Thomas Cartwright had just died—"schismatics, breakers of your laws; you may know them by their Turkey grogram." At the meeting the men of the Established Church of course wore their proper habits of office while the four Puritans showed their disdain for churchly garb by appearing in plain coarse fabric gowns. The Cartwright reference was serious because Cartwright had been the boldest of those who stormed against bishops; he thought the Church should have only elders. Worse, he thought the Crown should be under the Church. James knew well that the Church, with all its bishops, must be under him.

Rainolds was Bancroft's target because, it may be, Bancroft was loath to gibe at Chaderton, the other effective Puritan, who was his lifelong friend. Many of the learned men had long known each other. England at that time had only a few million people and ten thousand clergy, and friendships among scholars were widespread. Rainolds and Chaderton had gone to Cambridge together, and in a Town and Gown brawl Chaderton had saved Bancroft's life, nearly losing his own right hand to do so. Of the other two Puritans present, Thomas Sparke sat and said nothing while the fourth, John Knewstubs, "spoke most affectionately but confusedly."

The royal ire rose first at Rainolds, though later the king learned to endure him. With his own party Rainolds lost some esteem because they considered that, awed by the place and the company and the arbitrary dictates of his sovereign, he fell below himself. But the king made his angry opposition clear. Sir John Harington, the genius who invented the privy, was present and wrote to his wife that "the king talked much Latin and disputed with Doctor Rainolds, but he rather used upbraidings than arguments. .... . The Bishops seemed much pleased and said his majesty spoke by the power of inspiration. I wist not what they mean, but the spirit was rather foul mouthed."

As the crossfire increased and the meeting got rougher, perhaps the king saw that a diversion was wanted and seized upon Rainolds' one acceptable proposal to heal the breach. Or perhaps James, who thought of himself as a gifted Bible student, was sincere in seeing the need for a new translation even though the idea was advanced by the wrong side. Elizabeth before him had given some support to those who wished to see the Geneva Bible supplanted. James himself as a young man had tried his hand at making verses from the Psalms, and had written a commentary on Revelation.

The English people were Bible readers. Even before Wycliffe's Bible, the first in English, had enabled those who could read to know the Scriptures, early pieces in English had gone from hand to hand. The Wycliffe translation from the Latin text of the Vulgate was the foundation of Protestant thinking in England, its survival under ban and circulation in manuscript copies proof that the new Church was based upon a religious revolution and not merely the whim of a king determined to have a divorce the Pope forbade. An English Bible was one to be read by the common people. Educated men, high churchmen and

[7]

university scholars and royal persons, not only read Latin easily but wrote and spoke it with ease. Their private prayers, not merely those of the Church, were in Latin; so were addresses to the king. As a boy in Stirling Castle, the young James who would grow up to be king of both Scotland and England complained that they tried to make him learn Latin before he knew Scots. The tongue of the Church was useful as a common language for visitors from foreign lands, provided they were of the educated class. But the same class distinction kept the common folk who knew no Latin from reading the Bible.

William Tyndale was first to undertake a printed English Bible. Having studied under the great Erasmus at Cambridge, he began translation of the New Testament—from the original Greek and not the Latin translation. At first he hoped to get help from the Bishop of London, but Henry VIII and his bishops were not yet willing to let the people read. In 1524 Tyndale went abroad, a virtual exile, first to Germany where he saw Luther at Wittenberg and made arrangements to have his New Testament translation printed at Worms, using funds given him by a London merchant.

Proscribed by Henry VIII, the first English New Testament to be printed had to be smuggled into the country, and what copies could be seized by the authorities were burned. At Marburg, Germany, Tyndale proceeded with Old Testament translations, and with books that set forth Reformation doctrines. Henry VIII meanwhile, although he had left the Roman Church, demanded that Tyndale be returned to England to be punished for sedition. Tyndale remained on the Continent but at Antwerp in 1535 he fell into the hands of Emperor Charles V, who thrust him into a dungeon near Brussels. He was shortly sentenced as a heretic, and died at the stake. His last prayer was, "Lord, open the King of England's eyes."

Not all the Tyndale New Testaments were burned, and

enough of them reached England, beginning in 1526, to make it certain that one day there would be an English edition. In 1535, the year of Tyndale's death, Miles Coverdale edited and produced on the Continent the first complete English Bible, based on Tyndale, the Vulgate, and Luther's and Zwingli's translations. As Coverdale was a diplomat, he dedicated the book to Henry, and had no trouble with English publication. However, the Coverdale Bible was popularly known as the Bugs Bible because of its reading of Psalm 91:5: "Thou shalt not nede to be afraid of any bugges by night." Two revised editions appeared in 1537, carrying "the King's most gracious license."

Still another Bible, more closely related to Tyndale's pioneer work than Coverdale's, appeared in 1537—the so-called Matthew's Bible. This Bible also obtained a royal license and in, a large folio edition published in 1541, called the Great Bible, was read in churches. But the household Bible of the English people was the one produced at Geneva in 1560, mainly translated by William Whittingham, who married Calvin's daughter. Its popularity was due in part to its size—it was small enough to hold, while the church Bibles measured more than fifteen inches long and nine inches wide. Aside from its size, the Geneva Bible found favor among the followers of Calvin and Knox, but others found fault with its marginal notes and also with its wording. It was called the Breeches Bible because its reading of Genesis 3:7 was "and they sewed fig leaves together, and made themselves breeches."

At the time of the Hampton Court meeting, most Protestants, especially the Puritans, still read and defended the Geneva translation. In slurring it, James may have thought to balance his agreement with Rainolds by nettling them. Yet at least one rampant Puritan, Hugh Broughton, the famous Hebrew scholar, had called for a new Bible. As for the bishops, fifteen of them, as far back as 1568, had worked on a revision in the Bishops' Bible.

They had failed, however, to win royal sanction for their version, known as the Treacle Bible because it asked in Jeremiah 8:22, "Is there not treacle in Gilead?"

James's real reason for objecting to the Geneva Bible was rooted in his need to feel secure on his new throne. Some of the marginal notes in the Geneva version had wording which disturbed him: they seemed to scoff at kings. If the Bible threatened him, it must be changed. Away with all marginal notes! And indeed if you read them in the fat Geneva volume you will find many based on dogma now outworn. James may have had some right on his side; he was far from witless.

So clever indeed was his handling of the meeting that, although he gave the Puritan pleaders no satisfaction and actually threatened to harry them out of the land, he appeared to some observers to lean toward them. Indeed, the dean of the chapel said that on that day the king played the Puritan.

For their part the Puritans, with outward meekness and inner grumbling, found grace to yield enough to stay well within the Church of England. Yet after all the talk ended, it seemed they had won nothing. Indeed there was only one gain: the new Bible.

Having spoken, James went on about his royal business, which had nothing to do with translating Scriptures. At Royston, not far from Cambridge, he was converting a priory mansion and two old inns, set in six hundred acres, into a royal shooting box. Royston he came to esteem beyond all places for the hunting of hares, rabbits, partridges, bustards, and plovers. But the king hunted at Newmarket too, where also there was horse racing. When he had to return to town for the first Parliament of the new reign, he occupied the new royal apartments in the Tower of London and there, in the Lion's Tower, the king watched three dogs set upon a lion, which tore two of them apart.

Time to decide about the Bible had to be found between

these duties and pleasures, but the king knew how to delegate power. As soon as James showed approval of Rainolds' proposal, the ambitious Bishop Bancroft suppressed his own adverse thoughts and prepared to carry out the royal will with zeal and dispatch. Robert Cecil, who had served Elizabeth, served James as well; James called him "my little beagle" and made him Lord Salisbury. With Cecil, Bishop Bancroft talked things over and chose the men to work on a proposal, perhaps casually broached, which the royal will had now raised to a splendid design. Tyndale's prayer was now answered in full: James I had ordered what Tyndale died to do.

Fervent for what his master wished, Bancroft wrote to an aide: "I . . . move you in his majesty's name that, agreeably to the charge and trust committed unto you, no time may be overstepped by you for the better furtherance of this holy work. . . . You will scarcely conceive how earnest his majesty is to have this work begun."

# CHAPTER 2

# *Bishops' Move*

The King James Bible came about partly because forceful men thought they could use the project to further their private aims. In London, when the plague abated, old Archbishop Whitgift caught cold going from Lambeth Palace to see Bishop Bancroft at Fulham. Next, dining at Whitehall, he had a stroke and on the last day of February, 1604, he died. This was Bancroft's opportunity for promotion to the archbishopric, and he seized upon it with eager energies.

Of the ways to win James's approval, the new Bible might well be one. The task would certainly employ many of influence within the Church; among those present at Hampton Court on the day Rainolds made his speech were half a dozen—William Barlow, John Overall, Thomas Bilson, Thomas Ravis, Richard Edes, and Lancelot Andrewes—well able to grapple with the work. Good churchmen all, they toadied to James yet got along with Rainolds and his Puritan supporters.

In the summer of 1604 Bancroft was busy writing to the other bishops to announce that the king had "appointed certain learned men . . . for the translation of the Bible," and to ask that others be nominated. The bishops were required to inform themselves of all men learned in the Bible tongues within their districts. The king wanted to know of all who had "taken pains in their private study of the Scriptures," who could clear up places that were obscure in the ancient texts, and correct mistakes in former English versions. The bishops would report their findings to Mr. Lively, "our Hebrew reader in Cambridge, or to Dr. Harding, our Hebrew reader in Oxford, or to Dr. Andrewes, Dean of Westminster." Thus the translation would have the help of "all our principal learned men within this our kingdom."

When learned men had been appointed to the number of four and fifty, it became necessary to think about paying them. Of the fifty-four, some had no preferred places in the Church, or else had "too little for their deserts." Since the king could not "in any convenient time" give them more, he asked Bancroft to inquire about any vacant prebends [1] or livings worth twenty pounds a year or more which might be saved for the learned men. The king would reserve for one at work on the Bible any vacant office within his own gift; the Archbishop of York and the bishops in the metropolitan see of Canterbury, which still had no head since the death of Whitgift, were asked to do the same. Bancroft's reward was royal authority to write letters, surely a sign of preferment to come.

But the king wanted more learned men, even after he had named the fifty-four, and the handing out of livings alone would not suffice to pay them. In a letter to the Bishop of Norwich written on the last day of July, 1604, Bancroft had to propose that the prelates and clergy subscribe to the cost of the new Bible. The king, he said, was ready to bear "from his own princely disposition" the charges of some learned men, although it was only too well known that the Crown was hard up. Bancroft prayed his brethren the bishops, and each single dean and chapter, to give. "I do not think," he wrote, "that a thousand marks

[1] A prebend was that part of a church's income granted to a canon or member of the chapter as his stipend. Twenty pounds then would in purchasing power equal a thousand dollars or more now.

will finish the work." A mark was about two-thirds of a pound.

Although Bancroft added that he would acquaint the king with how much each gave, the bishops, deans, and chapters showed no quick zeal in sending money. In fact, it seems fair to say that the scheme fell through, for nothing further of it has come to light. Bancroft's estimate of costs must have been far too low. The scholars struggled along on their own means, though Oxford and Cambridge and Westminster seem to have given them free board and room when they were at work.

Of the three named to receive the reports of bishops and deans in the search for learned men, two, Lively and Harding, were Hebrew scholars at the two universities. Dr. John Harding, the rector at Halsey near Oxford, had been proctor of the university and in 1608 he was elected president [2] of Magdalen College by a unanimous vote. The unanimity suggested a recommendation from the king, as one of the awards promised translators. But Magdalen had seethed with unrest since the days of Elizabeth, and the vote of confidence in Harding could have been a protest against the policy of his predecessor, put in at the queen's request "to reform late decays and disorders." That election had been far from unanimous, in a college regarded as a "nursery of Puritans" in its objections to vestments and ritual. Harding's election marked a return of the Puritans to power, and during his two years of administration many "poor scholars" were admitted, the admission of commoners being part of Puritan policy.

Edward Lively, who for nearly thirty years had held the regius chair of Hebrew at Trinity College, Cambridge, was a man of all work—he had to be, to survive. Born about 1545, he studied Hebrew at Trinity under the noted John Drusitus, and married Catherine, daughter of Thomas

[2] President, provost, master, or warden all were used as titles for the heads of various colleges.

Larkin, M.D., who occupied the regius chair of physic. She bore him thirteen hungry children.

Then as now, the rewards of college teaching consisted largely of the feelings of well-doing, honor, and hope. To feed the family, Lively eked out his earnings with hack writing; the publisher Samuel Purchas said that he was one of his anonymous writers for his great series of *His Pilgrims*. In 1597 Lively signed and published *A True Chronology of the Times of the Persian Monarchy*, a work written in a quaint but hardly graceful style. Although it contained a random speculation about the nature of the locusts eaten by John the Baptist, it had little connection with the Bible.

Not even by his writing efforts could Lively make a living for his household. Once he sold his precious books to a bishop for three pounds. The most forlorn of all the learned men, the one for whom we may feel most sorry, he was never clear of suits at law or other disquieters of his study. He once had his goods distributed and his cattle driven off his ground, like Job's; he "led a life which in a manner of speaking was nothing else but a continual flood of waters," and even "his deer, being not so well able to bear so great a flood as he, even for very sorrow, presently died." Clearly his was a "lamentable and rueful" case, though such was the lot of many a scholar in England at that time.

Perhaps Lively's troubles made him patient; in contrast with most scholars, he was said to be a humble man who often suffered the foolish gladly. By the time the king made him a sort of drudge in the Bible task, his greatly burdened wife had died, leaving him eleven surviving offspring. Surely he needed preferment in accordance with the plan, and on September 20, 1604, he must have been grateful to get the living at Purleigh in Essex, fairly near to Cambridge.

The third member of the committee to sift recommendations, and the most important, was very different; he was the Dean of Westminster, supreme in the affairs of the abbey and subject to no higher prelate. Dr. Lancelot Andrewes had been among the highest of the high churchmen at the Hampton Court meeting. Now he was to become the real head, or chairman, of all those chosen to revise the Scriptures.

Andrewes was a man for all to like, and one whose fame has lasted. There are over a million words by and about him in print, and a volume of his sermons has lately been reissued. For the Anglo-Catholic he is almost a saint; T. S. Eliot wrote an essay, "For Lancelot Andrewes." Among the churchmen who were to translate he was the strongest, but the most graceful and polite, foil to the Puritans.

Andrewes was born in the parish of All Hallows, Barking, in 1555. A contemporary biographer wrote that his father, Thomas Andrewes, was a merchant who for most of his life "used the seas." Lancelot went early to the Coopers' free school at Ratcliff, and then to the well-known Merchant Tailors' school. "From his tender years," the biographer testified, "he was totally addicted to the study of good letters." Andrewes "studied so hard when others played that if his parents and masters had not forced him to play with them, all the play would have been marred." As a young scholar at the university, "he never loved or used any games of ordinary recreation, either within doors as cards, dice, table chess, or abroad as bats, quoits, bowls, or any such, but his ordinary exercise and recreation was walking, either alone by himself or with some other selected companion, with whom he might confer or argue, and recount their studies." Once a year, before Easter, he walked the thirty miles home to Barking from Pembroke College, where Sir Francis Walsingham helped in his support. One of the friends with whom he walked and talked was Edmund Spenser.

Did Spenser affect at all the writing style of Andrewes,

and through him that of the King James Bible? To such questions there can be no present answer. We do know that later Francis Bacon, his friend for twenty years, asked Andrewes' advice on writing. And we know that the great poetry of the age was all around the scholars as they worked on the Bible, was in their thought and feeling, and quickened the flow of their language.

Though he was no Elizabethan Wordsworth, Andrewes observed and loved the tamer kinds of nature: "He would often profess that to observe the grass, herbs, corn, trees, cattle, earth, water, heavens, any of the creatures, and to contemplate their natures, orders, virtues, uses, was ever to him the greatest mirth, content and recreation that could be." This penchant for common nature showed in his own writings and perhaps through some Bible passages in which he had a hand.

On his walks along the highways from Barking to Cambridge Andrewes must have seen the rogues who had long wandered there, the tinkers and peddlers, the wild homeless boys, the rufflers or holdup men and beggars, the minstrels singing and selling coarse ballads, the vagrant former soldiers. About these, pamphlets by Thomas Dekker and others, most of them with second-hand knowledge, appeared while the work on the Bible went on and may have helped Andrewes and the other translators cope with the scriptural censures of evil people.

After he finished his courses at Pembroke, young Andrewes became the catechist, giving lectures on the Ten Commandments at three o'clock on Saturdays and Sundays. People came to hear him from other colleges and from the country round about; they made notes and passed them on to friends. Thus samples of his early lectures are still extant.

On the command to make no graven images, Andrewes said, "Though God the law-maker appointed the representation of cherubim and of the brazen serpent, yet may not man presume to devise the like; he must take such resemblances as God himself gave him, and not of his own invention propound any." Unless of course, he added, God should direct him as He directed Moses.

Of "Thou shalt not take the name of the Lord thy God in vain," Andrewes spoke to distinguish between oaths and vows, and between those necessary and those voluntary. He dealt with swearing in a later sermon. Throughout his logic was clever, like that of the earlier schoolmen; and to the words of Scripture, though of course he believed them all, he applied what he thought was a divine common sense. He knew for instance that certain work must proceed on the Sabbath, and made strenuous effort to reconcile the Decalogue with the law of nature which, he said, was the image of God. Thus of killing he found that beasts have no right of society with us, because they lack reason. It cannot be a sin to use them for the end for which they were ordained: the less perfect for the more perfect, herbs for beasts and both for man. In the Bible God ordered a lot of killing, so to Andrewes it would have been foolish to say that God forbade the taking of any life.

Of the commandment to honor father and mother, he said we should all know what honor is and where it is due. God had not made all men alike, but made some partakers of His excellence and set them in superior places, others after a meaner degree and set them in a lower place, that society might be maintained. Did God create men equal? Surely not.

After Pembroke, Andrewes was chaplain to his patron Walsingham and to Archbishop Whitgift, and later rector of St. Giles in London's Cripplegate. In 1586, when he was only thirty-one, he was made one of the twelve chaplains to Queen Elizabeth, who loved having young men around her. She found Andrewes humane, cordial, gracious, benign, and took delight in the grave manner of his preaching.

Of this preaching there are varied reports. One said that he was an angel in the pulpit. T. S. Eliot said he took a word and derived the world from it, and ranked his sermons with the finest English prose of their time or any time. Yet some of his contemporaries said his style was jerky, with too much word play, too many conceits, quirks, puns. He was learned but did play with his text as a jackanapes does, who takes up a thing and tosses it. Witty, he was sometimes satirical; yet Thomas Fuller said that he had a guileless simplicity both of manner and mind, an unaffected modesty and a rare sense of humor.

We have Andrewes only on paper; in action he must have had a charm of delivery that we fail to find in the printed words. A biographer who had been his secretary, Henry Isaacson, said that God blessed his painful preachings; painful, in those days, meant taking pains.

Besides preaching Andrewes loved to manage. In 1589 he became Master of Pembroke Hall, where he managed to pay off the college debts and have a surplus. Such capability would be useful in directing the Bible work.

Andrewes also loved teaching and when in 1601 Elizabeth made him Dean of Westminster, he often took charge of the Westminster School in his own person. The young students were his special care. "What pains Dr. Andrewes did take both day and night. . . . He did often supply the place both of the head school master and usher for the space of a whole week at a time, and gave us not an hour of loitering from morning to night. . . . He caused our exercises in prose and verse to be brought to him, to examine our style and proficiency. . . . He never walked to Chiswick for his recreation without a brace of this young fry, and in that wayfaring leisure had a singular dexterity to fill those narrow vessels with a funnel." Thrice a week or oftener he called the uppermost scholars to his lodgings from eight till eleven at night, unfolding to them the rudiments of Greek and the elements of Hebrew grammar;

he was a night worker and said they were no true scholars who came to speak with him before noon.

All this he did, they said, without compulsion or correction; "Nay, I never heard him utter so much as a word of austerity among us." So we get glimpses of the rigid, but on the whole kind, schooling of the English divines.

Andrewes was with Elizabeth when she died and preached when she was buried. Then he aided in the Abbey rites at the coronation of James. The new king admired him "beyond all other divines, not only for his transcendant gift in preaching, but for his excellency and solidity in all kinds of learning." Fuller said, "His gravity in manner awed King James, who refrained from that mirth and liberty in the presence of this prelate which he otherwise assumed to himself." Yet Andrewes' smiling face in a portrait suggests his own very real sense of humor.

One of the rarest linguists in Christendom, Andrewes knew fifteen languages, and was so skilled in all of them, especially the Oriental ones, that Fuller suggested he might "almost have served as an interpreter general at the confusion of tongues." In writing he was tireless, using an amanuensis only to transcribe that which he had first written in his own hand.

Many thought him most fit to succeed old John Whitgift as Archbishop of Canterbury. King James, under the eye of Richard Bancroft who was already acting in Whitgift's place, delayed in raising anyone to that position. The king liked Andrewes but had to depend more on Bancroft, who threw his weight about and was less easygoing with the Puritans.

While Andrewes valued a high ritual, he never forced it on others. He had the highest scruples in giving preferments to the clergy, abhorred simony and strove always to find the fittest man for any place he had to fill. He had a wide knowledge of scholars throughout England and good judgment in weighing their talents. In short, this thoughtful walker possessed the traits most useful in choosing the men to make over the English Bible, and in welding them into a working unit.

Scholars and preachers were then poring over all portions of the Bible and writing on all the texts. Though the king had named fifty-four learned men, he intended many more to share in the work. Some lists today name only forty-seven but I have found more than the fifty-four, if we include replacements for those who died. The final version contains contributions from countless unknown linguists.

Many who sought advancement buzzed around the new king with servile praises. For instance William Thorne, about thirty-three and Dean of Chichester at the end of 1601, royal Hebrew reader at New College, Oxford, and greatly skilled in the sacred tongues, wrote and printed his *Kenning Glass for a Christian King* based on the text "Behold the man." Though Thorne's mirror for the perfect monarch repeated the Pauline advice against "acceptance of persons," of course James was flattered and made Thorne one of the learned men.

Thorne's name has never appeared on the many lists of translators. That he belonged with the rest is proved by a paper, preserved in The Public Works Office, London, saying that Mr. Thorne, king's chaplain, "is now . . . very necessarily employed in the translation of that part of the Old Testament" being done at Oxford, and urging that the church promote him further, as "very good and honest." [8] Thorne, in fact, must have been one of the scholars early chosen.

Though many sought to be considered worthy, the nature of the design demanded men of proved ability. And so, although the new king would give his name to the new Bible, its translators were Elizabethans all.

[8] Manuscript, Public Records Office. London, 1606.

# CHAPTER 3

# *Puritans' Progress*

While the high churchmen were adding to their preferment by work on the new Bible, what of the Puritans who
had suggested it?

Rainolds, who made the proposal, was among the foremost scholars in Elizabethan and early Stuart England.
Those who knew him held him to be the most learned
man in England, pious, courteous, modest, kind, and
wholly honest, with a vast memory that made him "a living
library, a third university."

John Rainolds was born about Michaelmas, 1549, at
Pinloe near Exeter in Devonshire. The fifth son of Richard
Rainolds, a papist, he went to Corpus Christi College, Oxford, where he "wholly addicted himself" to the study of
the Holy Scriptures. As a young convert from the Roman
Church, he must have had many inner conflicts as he
escaped more and more from beliefs in which even as a
child he had been restive. Others were going through the
same experience; at Oxford as elsewhere it was a stirring
time of rebirth and reform. Most people had grown up in
families holding to the Roman Church.

Soon after he got his degree, Rainolds was named Greek
reader, and his fame grew fast from his lectures. Among
the students he tutored was Richard Hooker, who was to
write *The Laws of Ecclesiastical Polity*, a work of influence even today. Rainolds himself read all the Latin and

Greek fathers, and all the ancient records of the Church that he could come by. He studied Aristotle and wrote a commentary that was highly praised. Also he practiced a style of writing, later called Euphuistic after Lyly's *Euphues,* which was based on alliteration and classic patterns of formal balance.

In 1579 he wrote a report over six hundred pages long of his attempt—an assignment from Sir Francis Walsingham—to turn from popish ways a young man confined in the Tower of London. To the poor imprisoned papist Rainolds was kind after a fashion, since he had been born a papist too, but also firm and severe. The small differences between them he compared to "small holes in ships at the which a great deal of water will come in, enough to drown the ship if they have been left open as long as these have been in the ship of the church." Rainolds set down all that was said by both during long sessions in the Tower, in which he prayed "God give you both a soft heart and an understanding mind that you may be able wisely to discern and gladly to embrace the truth when you shall hear it." Alas, the stubborn prisoner spent "twenty days in irons for not yielding to one Rainolds."

In 1586 Rainolds began lectures founded by Walsingham, at twenty pounds a year, to confute Romish tenets. Many hearers came three times a week, and those who believed as he did thought that he was doing great good.

Next, in 1592, he began an assault on stage plays. In 1566 when Rainolds was a student at Oxford, Queen Elizabeth had paid a visit to the university. At Corpus Christi College a play composed for her was acted, with Rainolds, then seventeen, playing the role of a female. The queen enjoyed the performance, laughing much and thanking the author for his pains. Now, nearly thirty years after, Rainolds could not forgive himself for acting the part of a girl. Nearly all his pamphlet, "The Overthrow of Stage Plays," was about how unlawful it was for men to wear women's clothing and for people to see such shameful make-believe. To him unlawful meant against the Bible. Had not the law of God, in Deuteronomy 22:5, forbidden a man to put on woman's raiment? But for some years more the English stage would continue to present boy actors in women's parts.

Of the plays themselves Rainolds complained, "They meditate how they may inflame a tender youth with love, entice him to dalliance, to whoredom, to incest, inure their minds and bodies to uncomely, dissolute, railing, boasting, knavish, foolish, brainsick, drunken conceits, words and gestures." Later the Puritans were to close the theaters, which would open again in the reign of Charles II, more corrupt and obscene than ever.

After some show of reason Rainolds went on to attack other entertainment of the times. "You say that there is a time for sports, plays, dances, a time for earnest studies; the man consisteth not of one part alone; he hath a body as well as a mind. Time of recreation is necessary, I grant, and think as necessary for scholars that are scholars indeed, I mean good students, as it is for any." Yet, he argues, "in my opinion it were not fit for them to play at stool ball among wenches, nor at mum chance and maw [a card game] with idle loose companions, nor at trunks [a sort of bagatelle] in guild halls, nor to dance about the maypole, nor to rifle [gamble with dice] in ale houses, nor to carouse in taverns, nor to rob orchards." Stool ball was a sort of cricket, an Easter game played between men and women with, as stake, a pudding or omelet flavored with tansy juice in memory of the Passover bitter herbs.

Now in 1592 the queen was again at Oxford, and as she was leaving she sent for the heads of houses and others. Then she "schooled Doctor Rainolds for his obstinate preciseness, willing him to follow her laws and not run before them."

Yet despite his strictness Rainolds was credited with "a

sweet gift in preaching" and a sharp and nimble wit. Patient and full of vigor, he conversed with young students "so familiarly and so profitably that whatsoever, how often soever, how much soever men desired to learn from him in any kind of knowledge," they could daily draw it from his mouth "as an ever springing and never failing well."

In 1593 he became Dean of Lincoln, and six years later he changed places with the troubled president of Corpus Christi College. There he set about to reduce a long turmoil and to repair and make lovely the chancel, the library, the hall; also to improve the scholarships and chaplainships. "Our commons," he said of the college, "are I confess in many places slender and short of that which our good founders meant for us, which hath risen through the want of faithful stewards, yet nowhere is it so scant as that we are enforced to gather herbs to make pottage, or to feed on a few barley leaves." He complained rather of heads who took what was meant for others and devoured it, "as though our colleges were meant only for heads, not at all for members." In such pleas for the wider spreading of good he showed himself a man of sense.

Indeed, as a Puritan dean in the college where Puritans were strong, Rainolds mellowed. He was gentle and pursued what he thought a righteous mean, wearing the square cap and the surplice and kneeling when he received the holy bread and wine. So content was he that he declined the queen's offer to make him a bishop. He had gracious words in these days even for women: "Think you that your wives, children, and servants have no souls, or that they are given them only for this life, instead of salt, to keep their bodies from putrefying?"

Yet "bitter words were daily shot at him" in the controversy of the time, and in 1602, as he walked in London, in Finsbury Fields "an arrow whether shot purposely by some Jesuited papist or at random, fell upon his breast but entered not his body."

[ 25 ]

Such was the man, simple enough at heart, whom King James had asked to Hampton Court as the "foreman" of the Puritans, who there as if on the spur of the moment asked that the Bible be rendered afresh in English, the man who was now to have a large share in the task. In spirit he was an Elizabethan artist in words who aided not only in finding happy phrases and rhythms but in fixing what was good in the Geneva version and others before it. In his hands the Bible would be safe.

With him to Hampton Court had gone the beloved Laurence Chaderton. Chaderton was born about 1537 in Lancashire, far from Rainolds' Devon. His family, like Rainolds', was Catholic, and his father was wealthy enough to trust the boy's early education to tutors who allowed him to spend his time in country sports. Then an able and learned tutor gave him good papist training and tried, in accordance with the father's wish, to push him into law. But before the Inns of Court came Christ College, Cambridge; there the Puritans were strong and young Chaderton became a convert.

His father wrote to offer him thirty pounds a year to quit Cambridge: "Son Laurence, if you will renounce the new sect which you have joined, you may expect all the happiness which the care of an indulgent father can assure you; otherwise, I enclose a shilling to buy a wallet. Go and beg."

With quiet courage Laurence refused this melodramatic offer, choosing to go on as a Puritan, and obtaining a scholarship. He eked out his means with some teaching, and his father may have helped him a little in spite of the threat.

At Cambridge Chaderton studied Latin, Greek, and Hebrew, learned French, Italian, and Spanish, and indulged a taste for botany. More robust than Rainolds, he engaged with vigor in Town and Gown fights, yet was also grave, learned, and pious, with a strict regard for the Sabbath. He was credited with a plain but cogent way of preaching and a firm dislike of Arminianism, which set up free will against free grace and taught that predestination is conditional, not absolute. At St. Clement's, Cambridge, he started a series of afternoon lectures or sermons that continued for fifty years.

He also preached at Paul's Cross, which long stood in the northeast part of St. Paul's churchyard, in the angle between the choir and the north transept. Here it was that the Tyndale Bible was burned. You may look in vain for this landmark now, for they tore it down in the days of the Long Parliament.

In 1576 Chaderton had to choose between his Cambridge fellowship and marriage. He resigned in order to marry Cecilia, daughter of Nicholas Culverwell, the queen's wine merchant. It was a long, happy union, with one daughter. Few of those who revised the Bible for King James had wives. Chaderton's domestic arrangements included servants, to whom he was said to be kind; thus he never kept a servant from public worship to cook victuals, saying, "I desire as much to have my servants know the Lord as myself." Yet if a servant was at any time given to lying or any other open vice, "he would not suffer her to remain in his house though she do ever so much work." Besides this fitting concern for the souls and morals of those who served him, Chaderton was credited with showing "a living affection for the poor, which is a certain token of a sound Christian."

The Puritans asked both words and works, and in their conflict with the Establishment over preaching versus forms, they had a great desire for a preaching clergy of their own. At St. Paul's Chaderton had complained, as the Puritans commonly did, against "those who serve mortal and sinful men with simony, flattering words, and servile obedience, not lawfully to obtain one room in the vineyard of the Lord, but two, three, four or more places"— meaning those of the clergy who held two or more livings at once. Where, he asked, "are the lips of the ministers which do preserve knowledge, or those messengers of God, at whose mouths His poor people should seek His law? Nay rather, where are not whole swarms of idle, ignorant and ungodly curates and readers who neither can nor will go before the dear flock of Christ in soundness of doctrine and integrity of life?"

In 1583 Sir Walter Mildmay, brother-in-law of Walsingham, treasurer of the queen's household, and a defender of the Puritans in their battle with the bishops, offered to found Emmanuel College if Chaderton would be its head. The plan was for the fellows of Emmanuel not to stay in the college at peace with their endless studies, as too many did, but to go out and spread knowledge in all parts of the country. After the college opened, the queen said to Mildmay, "Sir Walter, I hear you have erected a Puritan founddation." He replied, "No, madam, far be it from me to countenance anything contrary to your established laws, but I have set an acorn which, when it becomes an oak, God alone knows what will be the fruit thereof."

Chaderton himself declared a dozen years later that he "neither publicly nor privately spake any thing either out of a study of contradiction or with any kind of speaking evil of any man, but only publicly to back and defend the true doctrine of the Church of England." Though he felt most friendly toward the extreme Puritan party, he had no scruples about the sign of the cross in baptism and other disputed forms, and never separated himself from the disciplines of the Church or the authority of the law. When high church critics complained that communicants sat during the Lord's Supper in Emmanuel College, he said that it was difficult to kneel by reason of the seats being placed as they were, but that they had some kneeling.

Someone had said that a Puritan was "a Protestant frayed out of his wits," but such men as Rainolds and Chaderton were not easily frayed. If they could not resolve the differences that divided them from those who clung to the old forms, they could find ways to work and points of agreement. About a right English Bible, grounded on a wide range of learning, there could be no real dispute. It could help the many with knowledge.

Such a Bible would have room for all persuasions among the countless shades of strife, from the Brownists' whom none defended to those who under Bishop Bancroft wielded the huge willful strength of men entrenched in power. The struggle with these last was thirty years old and would go on until some of those who wanted to cleanse the Church would sail across the sea as Pilgrims. But first, for the new Bible, the strife between factions would be healthy. The Bible has always thrived on turmoil.

Though their differences like their skills were Elizabethan, those of the several sides who joined in the work would produce a masterpiece to transcend their age. With nice balance they put much of themselves and the background of the times into it, while also keeping much of themselves and their background out of it.

That those who worked on the new Bible had varied points of view was, then, to be no stumbling block but instead to insure its having something for all. We may regret that the learned translators were divided by no wider differences: there were among them no Roman Catholics, Jews, or women. They were male Protestants, roughly or smoothly within the Church of England, and as such they thought in certain grooves. The marvel is that they did so well.

# CHAPTER 4

# The Westminster Groups

The learned men arranged to carry on their work of translation in groups convenient to the other duties which, for many of them, came first. There were six groups: two at Westminster, one for the Old Testament and one for the New; two at Oxford, one for each Testament; and two at Cambridge, one for the Old Testament and one for the Apocrypha.

The Westminster group of the Old Testament was headed by Lancelot Andrewes, and met in his pleasant deanery. It included John Overall, Dean of St. Paul's, Hadrian Saravia, John Layfield, Robert Tigue, Francis Burleigh, Jeffrey King, Richard Thomson, William Bedwell, and Richard Clarke, all Hebrew scholars, greater or lesser. I shall present here the chief of these men and tell briefly of the rest in a postscript at the end of this book.

John Overall, son of George Overall, was baptized in the cloth-making village of Hadleigh, Suffolk, some fifty miles from London, March 2, 1560. Within a little over a year he appears to have been an orphan. At the Hadleigh grammar school he was a sizar, or poor student, who served the master for his board and lodging. Two or three years later he moved on with the master to Trinity College. Grave and handsome, he was in 1592 vicar at Epping, beyond Epping Forest, in Essex. In 1596 he rose to the royal chair of divinity at Cambridge. Two years later, after some conflict about the choice, he became, at the queen's behest, Master of Catherine Hall there. For one who had been a poor boy it was a very rapid advance.

Yet from this, advancement was to come. In 1602 the queen, on the urging of Sir Philip Sidney's friend, Sir Fulke Greville, made Overall Dean of St. Paul's. He of course retained his post at Cambridge.

At that time St. Paul's was a peculiar problem, its state one far from ideal grace. The nave, called Paul's Walk, had long been a meeting and trading place for all sorts of rough, noisy people. In an uproar like that of swarming bees, men and women thronged there to exchange news, to buy and sell horses, servants, and all kinds of things, to pick pockets and to concoct lawless schemes. It was a place where fops showed off and women from the streets sought, found, and bargained with men. Thomas Dekker wrote of the scene:

What swaggering, what facing and out facing. What shuffling, what shouldering, what justling, what jeering, what byting of thumbs to beget quarrels, what holding uppe of finger to remember drunken meetings, what braving with feathers, what bearding with mustachoes, what casting open of cloakes to publish new clothes, what muffling in cloakes to hyde broken elbows . . . such trampling up and downe, such spetting, such halking, and such humming (every man's lips making a noise, yet not a word to be understoode) . . . foote by foote, and elbow by elbow, shall you see walking the Knight, the Gull, the Gallant, the upstart, the Gentleman, the Clowne, the Captaine, the Apple-squire (pander), the Lawyer, the Usurer, the Citizen, the Bankerout, the Scholler, the Begger, the Doctor, the Ideot, the Ruffian, the Choater, the Puritan, the Cutthroat, the Hye-man, the Low-men, the True-man, and the Thiefe . . . whilst devotion kneeles at her prayers, doth prophanation walk under her nose in contempt of Religion.

Indeed it seemed that in Paul's Walk all the evil folk mentioned in the Bible rambled and strutted. There the jostling, the shuffling, the swearing, the coney catching, the squeals and shrieks and guffaws, the whole smelly hub-bub, became so scandalous that Shakespeare in *Henry IV, Part II,* and Ben Jonson in *Every Man in His Humour,* make reference to this profanation.

Part of Overall's work as dean was to clean up this messy traffic. This he did rather quickly, for a time at least, while he rode between London and Cambridge. He also ex-tended his responsibilities by getting for himself the liv-ings at Algarkirk in Lincolnshire and Clothal in Hert-fordshire. He was one of those condemned by Chaderton and others for being "plural parsons" with several in-comes.

Now at the age of forty-four, just before he became a Bible translator, he felt able to support a wife. On April 16, 1604, at Mitcham, Surrey, he married the lovely Anne, daughter of Edward Orwell of Christ Church, London. Called "the greatest beauty of her time in England," she was the most recent bride among the learned men as the Bible translation got under way. Before it was done, her flighty conduct would occasion gossip.

Why Overall was placed in the Hebrew group at West-minster is unclear, for he knew little of that language, be-ing mainly a Latin scholar. Fuller wrote of him that on his appointment to preach before the queen, "he professed . . . that he had spoken Latin so long, it was troublesome to speak English in a continued oration." With no great fondness for preaching, he was content to quote the church fathers, and in general his views made him "a discreet presser of conformity." Thus he wrote, "If any man shall therefore affirm that . . . all civil power, jurisdiction, and authority was first derived from the people and disordered multitude, or either is originally still in them or else de-duced by their consents, naturally from them, and is not God's ordinance originally descending from Him and depending upon Him, he doth greatly err." Clearly Overall had no use for any sense of commonwealth, no belief that the people of themselves could evolve government.

Asked by the Earl of Essex whether a man might lawfully enjoy recreation upon the Sabbath after evening prayer, Overall thought that he might—that it was "necessary that both body and mind should have recreation, that a man may be so tedious and worn out in the service of God that he may not be fit for God's service." Thus the dean, with all his duties, seems to have thought that serving God might be wearing. Yet while he was vicar at Epping he had written of a common theological point with simplicity and almost evangelical zeal: "I was requested to come visit some of my parish that were sick, and coming I found them sicker in mind than body. The thing that troubled their minds, so they said, was this. They could not be persuaded that Christ died for them. Wherein, having by the comforts of the gospel, as I thought best, somewhat eased and persuaded them, I took occasion afterward in my sermon, for their sakes, to handle this point . . . Christ died for all men sufficiently, for the believer only effectually, as the sun that shineth sufficiently to give light to all, though it doth it effectually only to them that open their eyes; as water that is sufficient to quench all the thirsty, but doth it only to them that drink it; as physic that is sufficient to cure all maladies, but doth it effectually only where it is applied. So Christ, the sum of righteousness, the water of life, the heavenly medicine."

We may discount some of the praise of Overall because it is of the kind that the florid writers about these Elizabethan worthies gave freely to all. Yet he was a prodigious learned man, they said, learned and judicious, with a strong brain to improve his great reading, and accounted one of the most learned, controversial divines of his day, one of the most profound of the English nation.

As a translator it was easy for Overall to go from St.

Paul's to Westminster, a trifle over two miles. He could have gone by road or by Thames river boat. St. Paul's was under Richard Bancroft, Bishop of London. To what extent the ambitious bishop and the successful dean were jealous of each other can only be surmised, but Overall seems to have been enough in the Bancroft party to rise with him. He made himself deeply useful to the bishops by preparing a great volume of canons.

Like Andrewes and Overall, Dr. Hadrian Saravia approved the divine right of kings and the august functions of bishops. King James and Bishop Bancroft must have found him a wholly safe man, sound in doctrine and practice. He was "a terrible high churchman," one to exude the richer airs of Europe, for he was among the few learned men of foreign birth and training. Born in Artois in 1531 and therefore the oldest translator, Saravia had a father of Spanish descent and a Flemish mother. Both had become Protestants, so he had no popish childhood to outgrow.

After training for the Church in the Low Countries, Saravia took part in drawing up the Walloon confession of faith and founded the Walloon church in Brussels. Copies of the confession were given to the Prince of Orange and to Count Egmont, the leaders of the Low Countries' Protestants, on behalf of the Calvinists. At Leyden, Saravia was professor of divinity in the university and received the degree of doctor of divinity while he was pastor of the French Reformed Church there. No link appears between him and the Pilgrims or Brownists who fled from England to Holland and later sailed from Leyden to Plymouth, Massachusetts, after Saravia had left the Low Countries.

Before reaching England Saravia was pastor of a church at Guernsey in the Channel Islands. Oxford gave him the doctor of divinity degree in 1590. There, while serving as vicar of Lewisham in Kent, he was a prebend of Canterbury, Worcester, and Westminster. His great friend was Richard Hooker, Rainolds' student, who tried to lessen conflicts and became known as the seeker for the golden mean. Izaac Walton wrote that "those two excellent persons began a holy friendship increasing daily to so high and holy affection that their two wills seemed to be but one and the same. . . . They were supposed to be confessors to each other."

Much of Saravia's writing is in Latin, but in plain English he maintained the authority of the bishops by apostolic warrant, and his "Treatise on the Different Degrees of the Christian Priesthood," published in 1590, maintained that "by apostles are meant bishops," with Titus and Timotheus in their turn created bishops by divinely authorized ordination. He warned the clergy of Guernsey that to overthrow this primitive polity was "not so much to reform as to deform," and explained that "a sound form of government does not allow all to have equal authority for governing." Clearly he was a man who disliked change and distrusted novelty.

Thus, writing of the great value of the universities, he said that without these seminaries of all learning and virtue, "the refinements of society and civilization generally would vanish, and leave mankind to relapse into that wild state of the savages of America." Only three of the learned men seem to have mentioned America, then so vastly unknown, and Saravia appears to have looked upon the New World with distaste and horror.

A younger member of the Hebrew group at Westminster, Dr. John Layfield, had actually gone out with those daring men who enlarged England's pride by voyage to lands beyond the seas. Layfield, a fellow of Trinity College, Cambridge, fared forth to the West Indies as chaplain to the third Earl of Cumberland.

Dr. Layfield enjoyed the flaunting colors of the tropics, and described with childlike delight what he saw on the islands where he landed. His is the sole really mundane writing that we have by any of the translators; he was earthy where all the rest were lofty. His long account of the voyage to Puerto Rico may be read in *Purchas, His Pilgrims.*

The voyage was made in a spring late in the 1590's, some say 1596, others 1598. In May at the island of Dominica Layfield wrote: "By two in the afternoon we were come so near abroad the shore that we were met with many canoes manned with men wholly naked, saving that they had chains and bracelets and some bodkins in their ears, or some strap in their nostrils or lips. .... They are men of good proportions, strong and light limbed, but few of them tall, their wits able to direct them to things bodily profitable. . . . They have wickers platted something like a broad shield to defend the rain, they that want these use a very broad leaf for that purpose. They provide shelter against the rain because it washeth off their red painting, laid so on that if you touch it you shall find it on your fingers. . . . They saw their women as naked as we had seen their men and alike attired even to the boring of their lips and ears. Yet in that nakedness they discovered some sparks of modesty, not willingly coming in the sight of strange and apparelled men, and when they did come busy to cover what should have been better covered. . . ."

Though we can prove nothing by mere diction, there are many words in this passage that are found in the King James Bible: apparel, attired, discovered, nakedness, boring ears, covered, profitable. The rhythms of Layfield also may remind us faintly of those in the books on which he labored.

"The soil is very fat," he wrote, "even in the most neglected places matching the garden plats in England for a rich black mold; so mountainous (certain in the places where we came near the sea coasts) that the valleys

[*36*]

may better be called pits than plains, and withall so impassably wooded that it is marvelous how those naked souls can be able to pull themselves through them without renting their natural clothes. . . . These hills are apparelled with very goodly trees of many sorts. The tallness of these unrequested trees makes the hills seem more hilly than of themselves happily they are; for they grow so like good children of some happy civil body, without envy or oppression, as that they look like a proud meadow about Oxford, when after some eruption Thames is again couched low within his own banks, leaving the earth's mantle more rugged and flaky then otherwise it would have been."

Of Puerto Rico he wrote: "The soldiers which were found to lie abroad in the fields, when they awaked found as much of their bodies as lay upwards to be very wet. . . . A wolvish kind of wild dogs which are bred in the woods and there do go in great companies together . . . live off crabs . . . an animal, a living and sensible creature . . . these woods are full of those crabs. . . . Parrots and parakeets are here . . . I have ordinarily seen them fly in flocks. . . ."

More than Lancelot Andrewes even, Layfield observed details and set them down. About plants he was exact and charming.

"A woody pine apple is of an exceeding durance and lasting. The taste of this fruit is very delicious, so as it quickly breedeth a fullness. For I cannot like it in the palate to any (me thinks) better than to very ripe strawberries and cream, the rather if a man hath already eaten almost his belly full. . . . It groweth upon a bush like an artichoke."

About drinks, which intrigued all Elizabethans, he said: "The Spaniard hath two . . . sorts of drink, the one called Guacapo made of molasses (that is the coarsest of their sugar) and some spices; the other kind, and used by the better sort of them, is called Alo which is a kind of Bragget (honey and ale fermented together) with many hot spices. . . ." Of cassava juice he wrote: "Sodden, there is made a pretty kind of drink somewhat like small ale." This is the writing of one who imbibed all the drinks with taste and good cheer. Conceivably he later relished fixing in English the Bible passages about drinking.

The strange plantains impressed him. "These plantains are a fruit which grow on a shrub between an herb and a tree; but it is commonly called a tree of the height of a man, the stem of it as big as a man's thigh, the fruit itself of the bigness and shape of a goat's horn, it groweth yellowish and mellow being ripe either upon the tree or with keeping, and then eaten raw or roasted it is a good meat, coming near to the relish of an Apple-john [a new word when Layfield wrote] or a duson that hath been kept till it is over-ripe, saving that methought I still found some taste of a root in it, the meat of it is lapped up in a thin skin, which being scored the long way with a knife, delivereth what is within it. . . ." That is an early record of the banana, a word which dates from 1597.

"Their Yerva will not have me forget it. This herb is a little contemptible weed to look upon, with a long wood stalk creeping upon the ground, and seldom lifting itself above a handful high on the ground. But it hath a property which confoundeth my understanding, and perhaps will seem strange in the way of philosophers, who have denied every part of sense to any plant; yet this certainly seemeth to have feeling. For if you lay your finger or a stick upon the leaves of it, not only that very piece which you touched but that that is near to it will contract itself and run together, as if it were presently dead and withered, not only the leaves but the very sprigs, being touched, will so disdainfully withdraw themselves, as if they would slip themselves rather than be touched, in which state both leaf and sprig will continue a good while, before it return to the former great and flourishing form, and they say that so long as the party which touched it standeth by it, it will not open, but after his departure it will. . . . It must be more than sense, whence such a sullenness can proceed."

That is easy, zestful writing, fairly direct though loose. Compare it with the simple, exact, firm accounts of the temple and tabernacle in Exodus and I Kings. Of Dr. Layfield it is said that "being skilled in architecture, his judgment was much relied on for the fabric of the tabernacle and temple." [1]

In 1602 Dr. Layfield became rector of a great London church, St. Clement Danes, which stands amid a parting of the traffic in the Strand. There, near where the learned men worked on the Bible at Westminster, he stayed for years.

Like Dean Overall, not long before the translating began and doubtless because he too had achieved a good living, Layfield let romance into his life. On January 22, 1603, John Layfield, aged forty, was licensed to marry Elizabeth, widow of John Brickett. She seems at once to have melted into his background, for we have no further mention of her. When Layfield needed more money, Thomas Cecil, Earl of Exeter, wrote to his half brother, Robert Cecil, Earl of Salisbury, asking that the latter give the living at Gravely to his "well worthy" chaplain, Dr. Layfield. There is no record showing whether he got the place.

Another of the younger men in the Westminster Hebrew group, Richard Thomson, called "Dutch" Thomson, was born in Holland of English parents. In 1587 he took his B.A. at Clare Hall, Cambridge, and he received his M.A. degree from both Cambridge and Oxford. His living was at Snailwell, Cambridgeshire. Later his sponsor was

[1] Collin, *Ecclesiastical History*, 1852. Vol. VII, page 337. This is the only plain statement I have found about what wording any translator wrought.

Sir Robert Killigrew. A great interpreter of Martial's Latin epigrams, he was also called a "grand propagator of Arminianism," the anti-Calvinist way of thought developed in Holland.

Prynne said he was "a debauched drunken English Dutchman who seldom went to bed one night sober." Yet Richard Montague called him "a most admirable philologer." Few divines were averse to drinking, and few wholly abstained from it. "Dutch" Thomson is the only one of the learned men to whom any referred as drunken. But if he had what others may have thought too much by night, he arose in the morning with his head clear enough to go forward competently with the day's work.

William Bedwell was a far more famous scholar in England, where he was the father of Arabic studies. Arabic he held to be the "only language of religion" as well as the chief language of diplomacy and business, "from the Fortunate Islands to the China Seas." Born in 1562, Bedwell was of Trinity College, Cambridge, and traveled in Holland, where he went to Leyden to see the Arabic collections of Scaliger, the famous linguist. In 1601 he was rector of St. Ethelburgh's in Bishopsgate Street, London. Not only an Oriental scholar, he was a mathematician, with a notable library of books on mathematics and astronomy.

In a hack work called "The Survey and Antiquity of the Towns of Stamford . . . and Tottenham High Cross," he described the town of Tottenham as "compounded of a quadrate and triangle, which kind of figure is of Euclid and his scholars both Greeks and Latins called trapesoiden."

Still odder writing may be found in his *Mahomet Unmasked* and his *Arabian Trudgman.* A trudgman, he said, "signifieth an interpreter." But some of his interpretations may be questioned: thus he said of "sarrha, serra, or as the Spaniards do pronounce it sierra, a desert place, a wilderness. Sahara: the stony country, the sands; the same almost that sarra is, that is a wilderness of desert, untilled and uninhabited, by reason that it is nothing but rocks and overspread with sand." Would any modern scholar connect Sahara with *sierra,* which means a long jagged mountain chain, from the Latin meaning "saw"?

Among the learned men of course were preachers as well as scholars. Richard Clarke, a fellow of Christ's College, Cambridge, and vicar on the island of Thanet, beyond the mouth of the Thames, was one of the six preachers in Canterbury Cathedral. Also he preached in the famous metropolitan Church of Christ, Canterbury. His sermons show the shape of his thought and his popular style: "There are two sorts of atheism, mental and vocal . . . I pardon the mouth atheist. For he that shall openly say, There is no God, will ipso facto be thought beside himself. Or if he seem to have his wits, yet they that hear him will abhor him; they will stop their ears against his blasphemy, they will hiss at him, they will spit at him; his impious assertion shall not stumble any one. But the heart atheist that saith God is, but thinks it not, and lives accordingly, ungodlily, unrighteously, unsoberly . . . his sin is greater than his hypocrisy."

The Westminster Hebrew group seems to have been a truly balanced team. It glowed with Elizabethan fire that ran through Andrewes, the linguist with a good temper; Overall, the plugging workman; Saravia, who had solid Leyden training; Layfield, of the simple style, who had voyaged to America; Thomson the master of word roots; Bedwell, versed in Eastern tongues; and Clarke, the zealous preacher. These, with the lesser men of the group, could sit down in a stone room by the fire and discuss in placid, capable fashion the books of the Bible they were to translate.

Nearly all these men at Westminster were from the south of England, most of them holding livings in or near

London. They needed to be within a day's ride on horseback from their places to carry on this special work regularly.

But there the likeness ended, for all shades of opinion were to be found among them. "Dutch" Thomson the Arminian came naturally by his views, but Saravia the high churchman had studied at Leyden and what did he think of Jacobus Arminius? Strict Calvinists, of course, liked even less the Arminian softening of the doctrine of predestination, and at this time the conformists in the English Church were perhaps less rabid than the Puritans.

Yet it is clear that while they worked together, at least, these learned men with all their shades of doctrine bore with each other. In the Westminster Hebrew group were none who fought in the open. They could unite in their desire to contrive a good and useful Bible and to confirm themselves in the good will of the king and of Bancroft, the strongest moving force in the Church. At the same time they had their own inner urges toward rewards— better livings, honors, added money. How could they afford to fight among themselves?

The Greek group at Westminster translated the Epistles. Their head was William Barlow, Dean of Chester, whose account of the Hampton Court parley is our main source for what took place there. As Chester is a long way from London, Barlow must often have stayed away from his duties as dean.

William Barlow had studied at St. John's College, Cambridge. He was a fellow at Trinity Hall in 1590, and granted a degree of doctor of divinity in 1599. Meanwhile in 1597 he was rector of St. Dunstan's in the East in London. Chaplain to Archbishop Whitgift, he also preached before the queen as one of her chaplains. She praised his sermon on the plow, saying, "Barlow's text might seem taken from the cart, but his talk might teach all the court." At the 1601 convocation he preached a famous "barley loaf" sermon that the Puritans misliked. At Hampton Court he showed that he misliked the Puritans.

An important event of his career before he began to translate the Bible was his role at the execution of the Earl of Essex, February 23, 1601. Three chaplains, of whom Barlow was one, heard the condemned lord recite the Creed on the scaffold. Essex, so tall, so youthful-looking, so blond, clad in scarlet, lay down and after a moment gave the sign for the end by thrusting out his scarlet arms. The mighty axeman thrice raised the axe in a mighty curve and thrice smashed it down. He was so frightened that he first slashed the earl through the shoulder, then through the head, and at last through the neck in a fashion most grisly. Stooping, he lifted the bloody head, held it high for all to see, and roared as was his final duty, "God save the Queen!"

About kings and queens, Barlow was always sound. Thus he wrote: "It is the prudence of a prince which swayeth the scepter as the stern guides the ship." The king's body, he said, is "sacred by holy unction." Sacred providence, he declared, "is to keep kings' persons and their authority sacred; that is, free from touch of disgrace, or dismay of terror by any human power." King James greatly approved of him.

Others in this New Testament group were John Spenser, Roger Fenton, Ralph Hutchinson, Michael Rabbett, Thomas Sanderson, and William Dakins.

John Spenser had many livings. Son of John, gent., he was born in Suffolk in 1559. In 1577 he earned his B.A. degree at Corpus Christi College, Oxford, where he received his doctor of divinity degree in 1602. He was rector of Aveley and Ardleigh, Essex, of Feversham, Kent, of St. Sepulchre's, Newgate, and of Broxtourne, Hertfordshire, all close enough to each other for relatively easy travel. His wife was a sister of George Cranmer. Another close friend of Richard Hooker, he wrote the foreword to Hooker's most famous work, *Laws of Ecclesiastical Polity.* Spenser's flowing style carried figures of speech to great lengths. In his sermon at Paul's Cross, "God's Love to His Vineyard," he elaborated on the comparison of the Church to a vine rooted in Christ, warning the Church in elaborate metaphors which ranged from horticulture to climate, from fencing to irrigation.

Roger Fenton, one of the bright young men among the Bible scholars, was born in Lancashire in 1565 and became a fellow of Pembroke Hall, Cambridge. In 1601 he was rector of St. Stephen's Walbrook, and in 1603 rector of St. Benet's, Sherehog. Since in 1604 he was also chaplain to Sir Thomas Edgerton, the Lord Chancellor, he appears to have been favored by the elite of the state. As has been observed, many of the translators had patrons in high places.

Fenton's main printed work was *A Treatise on Usury,* in which he described what he called "the usury of nature, that most important and primitive increase which the earth yieldeth in fruits unto man for his seed sown." With this man must not meddle. Usury in terms of interest on loans was another matter; Fenton doubted its virtue even for the benefit of widows and orphans. Yet, though he deplored the multiplying coneys of this branch of finance, Fenton became the "painful, pious, learned and beloved" rector of Chigwell, in Essex—a living maintained by those who knew enough to invest wisely. In other ways also the ravens came and the manna fell for him, because he had friends among the lofty.

While the sermons of these worthies gather dust on their shelves, the English Bible, for us the word of our God, stands forever. How could such men as Barlow, Spenser, and Fenton have risen to the literary heights reached by the King James version? We may say in awe and in the words which they so miraculously managed to choose for St. Paul, "I am persuaded, that neither death, nor life, nor angels, nor principalities, nor powers, nor things present, nor things to come, nor height, nor depth, nor any other creature, shall be able to separate us from the love of God, which is in Christ Jesus our Lord."

# CHAPTER 5

# The Oxford Groups

At Oxford the Hebrew group, which worked on the Major and the Minor Prophets and on Lamentations, was headed by Dr. John Harding, who had just risen to be regius professor of Hebrew. With him were John Rainolds, Thomas Holland, Richard Kilby, Miles Smith, Richard Brett, William Thorne, and Daniel Fairclough. The group had frequent meetings in Rainolds' quarters at Corpus Christi College.

Americans often find it difficult to understand the college system of Oxford and Cambridge universities. In the time of King James, and for long before, each college had its own distinct philosophy and was not merely a place for students to live but a unit in which each one with his special leanings might feel fairly at ease. Colleges differed in way of life as well as thought. A head such as Rainolds at Corpus Christi might set the tone, but perhaps even more he expressed traditions long present, or developing trends.

How the translators may have differed because of their college ties is beyond present seeking, but what of Oxford itself? Not long before, the university had nurtured Sir Philip Sidney and Sir Walter Raleigh, and such notable Elizabethan writers as John Lyly, Sir Henry Wotton, Francis Beaumont, and John Donne. George Chapman worked at Oxford on his Homer. At Christ Church College, since 1599, young Robert Burton had been writing his massive, magic *Anatomy of Melancholy*. How much did Oxford's literary air inspire the translators?

One who may have been so inspired was Dr. Thomas Holland, who was at once urbane and hidebound, a thorough Calvinist, yet a prodigy in literature. Born in Shropshire about 1538, Holland was one of the older translators. He traveled abroad but took his degree at Exeter College, of which he became master in 1592. Although he often refused to act in accord with forms and rules, he opposed any novel doctrines or ways of worship. In public he maintained—in contrast with the views of Dr. Hadrian Saravia and of Bishop Bancroft—that bishops were no distinct order from presbyters (elders or clergy of a second rank) and not at all superior to them. But the bishops let him alone, as just Dr. Holland and harmless—a renowned old codger whom all Oxford loved.

Of Holland it was said that he was "so familiarly acquainted with the fathers as if himself had been one of them, and so versed in the schoolmen as if he were the seraphic doctor," and "so celebrated for his preaching, reading, disputing, moderating, and all other excellent qualifications that all who knew him commended him, and all who heard of him admired him." Even while he labored on the Bible he gave much time to fervent prayers and meditations, with an ever-growing ardor for heaven. His farewell to his fellows, when he went on any long journey, was—in Latin—"I commend you to the love of God, and to the hatred of popery and superstition."

Rainolds the Puritan, whom we already know as the father of the new Bible, would have had little use for Lyly or Beaumont or any Oxford dramatist. We have seen how he repudiated his own youthful play acting. Another serious scholar with his mind on sermons was Richard Kilby, who also sought to escape the errors of his past. Kilby was born of humble parents at Ratcliffe on the Wreake, in Leicestershire. He went to Lincoln College, Oxford, where he became a fellow, then rector in 1590, and a doctor of divinity in 1596. He repaired the library there, making new shelving, and gave it many of his own books. In 1601 he was a prebend of Westminster Abbey.

In his sermon on "The Burden of a Loaden Conscience," Kilby implied that he had liked to sin, and had the common pride at having been a sinner, like a modern reformed drunkard. Speaking of what he called his "reprobate heart, which being utterly hardened in sin, and void of repentance, causeth me to heap wrath upon wrath and vengeance upon vengeance to the increasing of mine overlasting torments in hell fire," he pleaded, "all manner of people, young and old, take heed by me. Have no more Gods but one."

For, he continued, "Consider well what He hath done for you. He made you at the first like unto Himself, in wisdom and holiness, and when you were by sin made like the devil, and must therefore have been condemned to hell torments, God sent His only son who taking unto him a body and soul, was a man and suffered great wrong and shameful death, to secure your pardon, and to buy you out of the devil's bondage, that ye might be renewed to the likeness of God . . . to the end ye might be fit to keep company with all saints in the joys of heaven." Today Kilby would be preaching a revivalist gospel.

In the same sermon he quoted his own bedtime prayer, in which he abased himself and at the same time seemed confident that he would be all right: "O most mighty and most gracious Lord God, I, wretched man, the worst of the world, do cry Thy mercy for all my sins, which this day or at any time have come out of my heart, by way of word, deed or thought. I heartily thank Thee for all the blessings which Thou has graciously and plentifully given me. . . ." He ended with a blanket petition: "Be merciful . . . unto all those for whom I ought to pray."

Kilby also left us some verses, which you will find in no volume of great Elizabethan poems:

> With truth, repentance and right faith
>     Mine heart and soul fulfil,
> That I may hate all wickedness,
>     And cleave fast to Thy will.

Yet there is some ground for thinking that Kilby was among the more precise translators, a stickler for the right word, the right phrase. His plain, direct prose style may have served those Old Testament prophets who in English needed something of his simple glow. We may think of him as well-equipped to render the dirges in the Lamentations, with their occasional words to lift us out of despair. "It is good that a man should both hope and quietly wait for the salvation of the Lord. . . . Thou drewest near in the day that I called upon Thee; Thou saidst, Fear not."

Miles Smith of this Oxford group was perhaps the most useful of all the learned men. In the end he went over the whole Bible as an editor, taking the greatest pains from first to last. He wrote the preface once printed in all King James Bibles, which deserves more reading today and ought to be bound into current editions. Yet Smith "was never heard to speak of the work with any attribution to himself more than the rest," and he wrote of his fellow translators, "There were many chosen that were greater in other men's eyes than in their own and that sought the truth rather than their own praise."

Like John Rainolds, Smith was a Calvinist who conformed enough to meet the Church of England halfway. We could hardly call him a Puritan. He made strong objection to sycophancy, but wrote in favor of churchmen's acceptance of their lawful fees. After his own ascent to a high place, he remained humble, and broke off a most serious discourse to see a poor minister who wished to speak with him, saying, "But he must not wait, lest we should seem to take state upon us."

Because he was the final critic who looked for flaws and smoothed out the whole translation, there is perhaps more of Dr. Miles Smith in the King James version than of any other man. Some critics said that his own style was heavy, involved, rough. Yet some of his writing showed a succinct grace, and clearly he had a good editor's sense of united effort when he wrote, in comment on Ephesians 5:18, "As in the play of tossing the ball, it is not enough for one of the players to be cunning in throwing of it, but the other players also must take it . . . handsomely, firmly, or else the ball will go down." Smith took "handsomely and firmly" what the others wrote; for that at least his literary skill sufficed. As one said of him, "He . . . set forth the new and exact translation. . . . He delivered the Scriptures . . . to Englishmen in English."

At the head of the Greek group in Oxford was Thomas Ravis, Dean of Christ Church. His colleagues were Richard Edes, Dean of Worcester; Sir Henry Savile; John Perin; Ralph Ravens; John Harmer; Giles Thomson; and George Abbot, Dean of Winchester. Their portion was the Four Gospels, the Acts, and the Apocalypse.

Of all the learned men only George Abbot reached the summit of an English churchman's desires on earth. He was also the only one of the translators who ever killed a man.

Thomas Ravis was haughty and harsh; at the Hampton Court meeting he spoke at some length against the Puritans. Born in Old Malden, Surrey, about 1560, he went to the Westminster school. In 1575, sponsored by William Cecil, Lord Burghley, he applied to Christ Church, Oxford, a college founded by Cardinal Wolsey and famous for its Gothic hall. There the dean and chapter declined to admit young Ravis for lack of room, and only a strong letter from Burghley got him in. Twenty years later he became a doctor of divinity, and in 1596 dean of the college. He was the first from the Westminster school to become a dean, and "always continued both by his counsel and countenance a most especial encourager of the studies of all deserving scholars belonging to that foundation."

Meanwhile Ravis had preached in or near Oxford "with great liking." Rector at Merstham, in Surrey, and of All Hallows Barking, he was in 1593 a prebend of Westminster. Thus he was of the inner circles among churchmen, among the fastest to rise in the Church, and a sharp foil to the Puritan Rainolds of the Hebrew group. As chaplain to Archbishop Whitgift, he had dealt sharply with the Puritan leader Cartwright.

While Dean of Christ Church, Ravis had administrative troubles when he compelled the members of the college to forego their "allowance of commons," that is, the customary meals at the college tables, in exchange for two shillings a week. Some who opposed the change he expelled, others he sent before the council, and others he put in prison. "A grave and good man," he was able at getting work done and considered a model for lesser folk to revere, but clearly not a man without choler. In retrospect we may think him an odd choice for chairman of the group to work on the writing that contains the heart of Christian teaching.

The most handsome of the translators was tall Sir Henry Savile, who had a fair, clear, rosy complexion as fine as any lady's. His portrait shows more round flesh than accords with our notion of a handsome man. He was born in 1549 at Over Bradley near Halifax, Yorkshire, a younger son without a square foot of land. After his studies at Brasenose College, Oxford, he traveled in 1578 through Europe, where he gained a general acquaintance with the learned men and through them obtained a number of rare Greek manuscripts. For a time he was tutor to Queen Elizabeth in Greek and mathematics. She liked him very much.

Then he was Dean of Carlisle and Provost of Eton. The most learned Englishman in profane literature of Queen Elizabeth's reign, Savile was thought by some to be "too much inflated with his learning and riches." As Warden of Merton College he was a severe governor, oppressed his young scholars grievously, and was duly hated by them. In a different sphere, he was skillful with gardens and cherished an orchard and a nursery of young plants.

Oddly, in view of his literary appreciation, Savile could not abide wits. When a young scholar was recommended to him as a good wit, he exclaimed, "Out upon him; I'll have nothing to do with him; give me a plodding student. If I would look for wits, I would go to Newgate; there be the wits.' If he preferred plodding to wit, he was wise in his own eyes and wholly correct in church doctrines. Like Saravia a friend of the serious Hooker, he translated the history of Cornelius Tacitus, gave learned lectures on Euclid, and edited the works of St. Chrysostom. About the latter work there was to be a rather unseemly row between two other Bible translators.

On September 21, 1604, Savile was knighted by King James at an Eton College banquet. Under James knighthood was no great honor; he awarded honors in large numbers, charging high fees in a sort of royal racket. A rarer gift came from Savile himself; he presented an early edition of the Gospels in Russian to the new Oxford library named for Sir Thomas Bodley. Also he founded two professorships, in mathematics and astronomy.

About Giles Thomson, Dean of Windsor, little is known beyond the fact that he was a fellow student of Lancelot Andrewes at the Merchant Tailors' school. Andrewes had

King *J*ames I of England and VI of Scotland, whose royal command in support of the Puritan proposal for a new Bible translation persuaded the bishops of the Church of England to approve the project.

Hampton Court, where the conference which sponsored new translation was held. The entrance gate pictured has been little changed since it was built by Cardinal Wolsey.

Title page from the first edition of the King James Bible, showing Moses (left), Aaron (right), and the gospel writers.

Doctor *John* Rainolds, Puritan, spoke at Hampton Court of the need for a new translation. Called the most learned man in England, Rainolds worked with the Oxford group that translated the Old Testament, but he died before the new Bible was completed.

IOANNES RAINOLDVS
Cum vivat docte Rainoldus fulmina lingue
Romanus tremuit Iupiter et merito

ard Bancroft, Bishop of
on, as a high churchman
sed Rainolds' Puritan
osals yet moved with en-
for the new Bible when
King approved. After the
of *John* Whitgift, Ban-
was rewarded with the
bishopric of Canterbury.

George Abbot, among the New Testament translators at Oxford, followed Bancroft as Bishop and became Archbishop in time to oppose the tyranny of Laud. His engraved portrait is from the title page of his book, *A Brief Description of the Whole World*, as published in 1656.

Lancelot Andrewes, Dean Westminster, chose m other translators and led Westminster group trans ing from the Hebrew. drewes had been a chapl to Elizabeth; he was a fri of Bacon and Spenser, young *John* Milton wrote elegy, when, in 1626, he d

Thomas Ravis, Dean of Christ Church and later Warden of New College, was head of the New Testament translators at Oxford. A high churchman, Ravis opposed Puritan teachings. He signed the document that asked promotion for another translator, Dean Thorne.

Sir Henry Savile, conside the handsomest of the tra lators, had tutored Qu Elizabeth in Greek and ma ematics. Provost of Eton, th Warden of Merton, he wor with the Greek group at ford, where he lectured on Greek philosophers and Eucl

Thomas Bilson, Bishop
Winchester, worked with
Cambridge translators a
was one of the two final e
tors. His high church vi
and zeal for the Establishm
balanced the Puritan leani
of Miles Smith, who follo
him in the see of Winches

Doctor Miles Smith worked in
the Oxford group that translated the Old Testament from
the Hebrew. He also served
as final editor of the whole
translation and wrote the eloquent preface, "Address to
the Reader," which was
part of the 1611 edition.

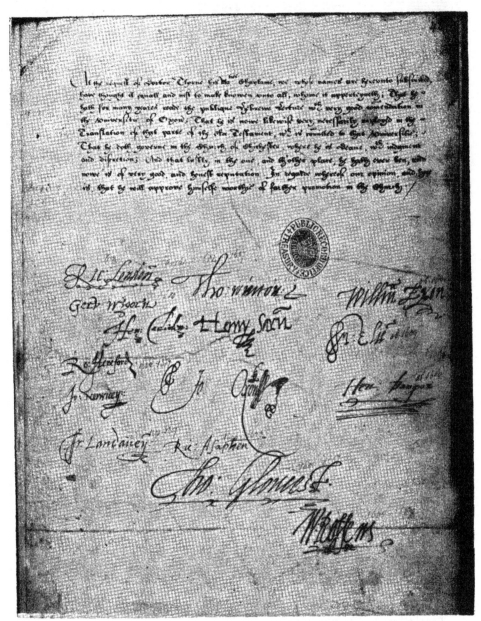

The Thorne Document, from the Public Record Office, London, proves that William Thorne, Dean of Chichester, was among the translators. In it others of the learned men petitioned for Thorne's preferment.

a wide knowledge of the scholars throughout England and good judgment in weighing their talents.

Passing over for the present those of this Oxford New Testament group about whom we know little, we come to George Abbot, the translator who in after years killed a man. He was born October 29, 1562, at Guildford, Surrey, some twenty miles from London, a son of Maurice Abbot, a clothier, and his wife Alice March. Both were staunch Protestants, good people, perhaps humdrum, but with longings for something grander.

When Alice March was pregnant in 1562, she had a portent of what was to come. She dreamed that if she could catch and eat a jack or pike, her child would prove to be a son, not a daughter, and would rise to the heights. Crafty as she drew water from the river hard by, she entrapped a young pike in her pitcher. By promptly cooking and eating the fish she fulfilled her dream; God must have given the pike to her. The birth of the boy was a holy event, a marvel to the good gossips of the town. Persons hearing of Alice's success, that she had improved the omen, offered to sponsor the boy and aided in his schooling. At sixteen George entered Balliol College, Oxford.

In 1597 he was a doctor of divinity and Master of University College. Many attended his sermons at St. Mary's, Oxford. Soon he was vice-chancellor of the university and Dean of Winchester. A man of morose manners and a sour aspect, he was prosy, pious, devout, a hard worker, always ready to assert firmly what he believed, but narrow of mind and full of rancor, in marked contrast to Lancelot Andrewes, who was his friend. Seeking to win the Puritans by sometimes preaching Calvinistic or Augustinian doctrines, he yet maintained the fixed order of the Church and was dogged in upholding the rule of the bishops.

Abbot published in 1599 *A Brief Description of the*

*Whole World.* In this work he wrote: "In very many parts of these northern countries of America there is very fit and opportune fishing some pretty way within the sea. . . . A huge space of earth hath not hitherto by any Christian to any purpose been discovered, but by those near the sea coast it may be gathered that they all which do there inhabit are men rude and uncivil, without the knowledge of God. Yet on the northwest part of America some of our English men going through the straits of Magellan and passing to the north by Hispana Nova have touched on a country where they have found good entertainment, and the King thereof yielded himself to the subjection of the Queen of England, whereupon they termed it Nova Albion. . . . They are marvellously addicted to witchcraft and adoration of devils, from which they could not be persuaded to abstain even in the very presence of our countrymen."

In 1599 there had been a flurry about witchcraft, more in Scotland than in England. King James had published his book, *Demonology,* in 1597, the year in which he stopped the worst of the Scottish witch hunts, which had been rampant since 1590. The clamor about witchcraft had already lessened in England. Until comparatively modern times witchcraft had been rife in all ages and in all places; the Old Testament, as we know, has many references to it. Abbot's mention of witchcraft in America indicates that, like most people, he believed in its existence and was against it. What seems to have stirred him about it as practiced by savages in America was that they had dared to go ahead with it in the presence of enlightened Englishmen.

There is nothing to be found in Abbot's book more lively than the passage quoted. What he wrote was secondhand, and his style was dull, though it sufficed for what he had to say. One more sentence has contemporary interest: "The manner of government which of late years hath been used in Russia is very barbarous and little less than tyrannous."

At University College in 1600 he gave "An Exposition upon the Prophet Jonah," one of "those lectures which with great solemnity are kept both winter and summer on the Thursday mornings early, where sometimes before daylight the praises of God are sounded out in the great congregation." In this he said: "They rowed to bring the ship back unto the land. The word which is used here . . . in the Hebrew doth signify they did dig, either because men do thrust into water with oars as in digging they do with other instruments on the land . . . or because as men in digging do turn this way and that way and stir and move the ground, so they stirred up their wits and beat their brains and thoughts to free him (Jonah) from the danger. . . . God hath so coupled all creatures to mankind, with a chain of strong dependence, that the being of them is much suitable to the flourishing or fading of the other."

Did the Oxford groups, in faith and devotion, dig and stir to free the Bible from obscurity? It may be hard for us to discern in gruff Ravis, stern Savile, and dull Abbot talents enough to convey to us all that we know of the loving-kindness of Christ.

# CHAPTER 6

# The Cambridge Groups

At Cambridge the Hebrew group had as chairman Edward Lively, the father of thirteen children, whose weal and woe we have discussed. The others were John Richardson, Laurence Chaderton, Francis Dillingham, Thomas Harrison, Roger Andrewes, brother of Lancelot, Robert Spalding, and Andrew Bing. This group dealt with the books from I Chronicles through Ecclesiastes. To it, therefore, we are indebted for the Psalms.

Cambridge had given its degree to Christopher Marlowe, the free-thinking dramatist said to have been a "scorner of God's word," to whom "Moses was but a juggler," Protestants "hypocritical asses." Men, he said, most needed "not to be afraid of Bugbears." Other famous Cantabrigians of the era were Francis Bacon, Edmund Spenser, Thomas Campion, John Fletcher, Robert Greene, Thomas Lodge, and Thomas Nash, whom Cambridge expelled. Their lyrics fill the books of Elizabethan verse.

Campion's "Cherry Ripe" begins:

> There is a garden in her face
> Where roses and white lilies blow.

Yet he could write also sacred verses still read today:

Never weather beaten sail more willing bent to shore,
Never tired pilgrim's limbs affected slumber more,

Than my wearied spirit now longs to fly out of my
    troubled breast;
O come quickly, sweetest Lord, and take my soul to rest!

One of Thomas Lodge's famous lyrics begins:

> Like to the clear in highest sphere
> Where all imperial glory shines,
> Of selfsame color is her hair,
> Whether unfolded or in twines,
> Heigh ho, fair Rosaline . . .
> Heigh ho, would she were mine.

The love poems of the Song of Songs, which this Cambridge group put into English, are far more lush and concrete.

The poetry of the Bible has no rhymes, but is what we might call free verse, with balanced lines, mainly in couplets. Thus in Psalm 23 Cambridge gave us:

Surely goodness and mercy shall follow me all the days
    of my life,
And I will dwell in the house of the Lord for ever.

The Geneva Bible read:

Doubtless kindness and mercy shall follow me all the days
    of my life,
And I shall remain a long season in the house of the Lord.

Compare likewise the King James Bible's,

> I will lift up mine eyes unto the hills,
> From whence cometh my help,

with the Geneva Bible's,

> I will lift mine eyes unto the mountains,
> From whence my help shall come.

The Cambridge Hebrew group had a goodly knack with English words and sounds.

One fact that stands out about John Richardson of

Cambridge is that he was fat. Those of another persuasion called him a "fat bellied Arminian." As such he might have fought with Laurence Chaderton, the Puritan, but there is no record of conflict. These scholars bore and forebore. Thin, acrid men alone could hardly have done over the Bible to suit the fully fed.

John Richardson was born at Linton, seven miles from Cambridge, about 1564. The place and the date attest once more that these learned men were nearly all youngish or of middle age, and came from the regions about London, Oxford, and Cambridge. They were a cross section, not of the English people or even of the English clergy, but of the scholars who happened to be at hand for the venture. Richardson went to Clare Hall, Cambridge, where he must have known well Richard Thomson, "Dutch" Thomson, the other Arminian, with the reputation for drink. In 1595 he became rector of Upwell, Norfolk, and two years later was a doctor of divinity. A foremost Hebraist, he was also a popular theologian. He seems to have been one of those fat men whom most people like.

Francis Dillingham was born at Deane, Bedfordshire, went to Christ's College, Cambridge, and was a good linguist. Though he never married, he believed strongly in marriage for other clerics, and wrote much on a subject then the theme of argument in the English Church. In 1603 just before he started work on the Bible, he published *A Quartron of Reasons, Composed by Dr. Hill, Unquartered, and Proved a Quartron of Follies.* Dr. Hill had railed against Protestant ministers "being so much occupied about wooing, wenching, and wiving, taking upon them to be doctors of divinity and husbands too." Dillingham countered: "Papists teach that ministers may not have wives. Is this catholic? Many hundred years after Christ priests had wives."

Queen Elizabeth had allowed the clergy of the English

Church to marry. However fellows of the colleges, if they married, still were required to resign. Dillingham felt he had a message for those who fell into troublous thoughts about marriage. So he published *A Golden Key Opening the Lock to Eternal Happiness*. It is an earnest of the guides to good thinking, to peace of mind, soul and body, in our day. To be happy a man should simply keep his wife subject unto him.

"It is a principle in nature," Dillingham wrote: "marry with thy equals. By . . . unequal marriages, how many men have become subject to their wives? . . . May not men nowadays see wives on horses, and husbands walking as servants on the ground?" No Englishman with self-respect should stand that.

"That a man may obtain a wife that will be in subjection unto him," he went on, "he must choose a prudent and wise wife, for prudence and wisdom respecteth persons, place, and manner of doing a thing. . . . Prudence teacheth the wife that her husband is her head, and so subjecteth her self unto him. No marvel then though many men have not their wives in subjection, for they have married fools which know not their place. . . . A wise woman, saith Solomon . . . buildeth the house, but the foolish destroyeth it with her own hands." The King James version (Proverbs 14:1) says: "Every wise woman buildeth her house, but the foolish plucketh it down with her hands."

Dillingham went on: "He that will have a wife in subjection, let him match with a religious woman, for religion teacheth her subjection. Be not unequally yoked, saith St. Paul, II Corinthians 6:14, with infidels." (The King James Bible says, "yoked together with unbelievers.") "A man of religion," said Dillingham, "that matcheth with an irreligious woman is unequally matched, and therefore his yoke needs be heavy. A house divided cannot stand. How should that house then stand where man and wife

[*59*]

are divided, one drawing this way, another that way? . . . The misery of this age is that . . . men inquire after wealth, not after religion in a woman. Hence it is that some live discontentedly, and come in the end to great misery."

This was all sound advice from a young, wifeless man, who knew nothing of our modern equal rights for women. The viewpoint of Dillingham is often close to that of the Proverbs and Ecclesiastes which he helped to translate. What he himself published is wholly in accord with the male nature of the Bible and with the thought of his own age. Though Dillingham doubtless hoped his sermons would change the ways of love, unwise, luckless men have gone on wooing and wiving foolish females to this day.

. Though he argued in print with high churchmen, it would be wrong to think of Dillingham as a Puritan, for he conformed strictly to the Church of England. He was a typical Elizabethan except that he never indulged in profane love.

Thomas Harrison, who was indeed a Puritan, was born in London in 1555, and went to the Merchant Tailors' school, where he was second in learning only to Lancelot Andrewes. A graduate of St. John's College, and Master of Trinity College, Cambridge, he had exquisite skill in Hebrew and Greek idiom. The renowned Dr. Whittaker, for the excellence of his verses, called Harrison his poet. Such a man would have been of much service in the work on the Psalms. There was at least one poet among the translators, though none of his poems have survived.

Andrew Bing was a tall, smiling young man. Born in Cambridge in 1574, he went to Peterhouse, and then became professor of Hebrew in Trinity College, Cambridge. Later he was subdean of York for many years. Only thirty when King James chose him to work on the Bible, he outlived nearly all his fellow workers.

The New Testament group at Cambridge, headed by John Duport, included William Branthwaite, Jeremy Radcliffe, Samuel Ward, Andrew Downes, John Bois,[1] and a second man named Ward, Robert. It translated the Apocrypha, and in the long run might have seemed inconsequential, except that one of its members, John Bois, was a man fully worth knowing, who played an important part in the final revision of the entire Bible.

John Duport, son of Thomas Duport, Shepshed, Leicestershire, was a fellow of Jesus College, Cambridge, and then master. He earned his doctorate in divinity in 1590, and in 1595 became precentor of St. Paul's. His wife, doubtless well subject to him if his colleague Dillingham spoke for him, was Rachel, daughter of Richard Cox, Bishop of Ely. By her he had two sons, one of whom was also a noted scholar. Dr. Duport was a learned man of high standing in England.

William Branthwaite took his B.A. at Clare Hall, Cambridge, in 1582, and his D.D. at Emmanuel College in 1598. He was Master of Gonville and Caius College, Cambridge. An extant letter from Branthwaite to Sir Thomas Wilson, who had the ear of a lordly patron, begins with concern for the health of the recipient. Branthwaite wished that "my letters might bear bezoar or unicorn or some other more sovereign cordial either to cure your malady or to comfort against the fits and encounters thereof." Bezoar stone was a sort of charm against poisons, and though there are none of these stones in the Bible, they were, as Branthwaite shows, in the thought of the age. The mythical unicorn is found in nine Bible verses. Its horn, if one could have got it, would have been used to cast out poisons; the practice of doctors in those days was still largely magic.

"There be three physicians," Branthwaite went on,

[1] Often spelled Boys and evidently so Anglicized in pronunciation.

"which the state of your body (if I mistake not) requires should always attend you and they are as good fellows and friends as physicians . . . Dr. diet, quiet, and merry man. . . . Under diet I also comprehend those other things which the art and language of physicians express thereby as change of air, moderate exercise, and proportionable sleep, and the rest. For the first methinks it should be very convenient for you both to refresh spirits and to confirm and continue health, especially some little remove out of London now and then in the hot months of July and August. . . . Many times it falleth out that a strong mind endangereth a weak body." In this letter Branthwaite was seeking an advance for himself and aid for his college, in the best fawning manner of scholars of the time.

Samuel Ward, son of John, of Durham, was a timid young Puritan, early intent on putting down his own sins. He was born in 1577, went to St. John's College, Cambridge, and was fellow at Sidney Sussex College in 1599. In 1603 he was town preacher at St. Mary's le Tower in Ipswich. The next year he married Deborah Bolton, a widow, of Isleham, Cambridgeshire. At college he kept a diary, still extant, which reminds us a bit of the young Boswell. Apparently he was the youngest of the translators.

On May 13, 1595, in his diary he condemned himself for "My desire of preferment over much." Often he addressed himself in the second person. Thus that same day he wrote, "Thy wandering regard in the chapel at prayer time." May 17, "Thy gluttony the night before." May 23, "My sleeping without remembering my last thought, which should have been of God." May 26, "Thy dullness this day in hearing God's word . . . thy sin of pride . . . thy by-thoughts at prayer time same evening." June 14, "My negligence . . . in sleeping immediately after dinner . . . in hearing another sermon sluggishly." June 12, "My too much drinking after supper.' June 22, "My immoderate diet of eating cheese." June 27, "My going to drink wine, and that in the tavern, béfore I called upon God." July 8, "My immoderate laughter in the hall." July 15, "My incontinent thoughts at Hobson's."

The next year young Ward wrote, July 19, 1596, "My gluttony in eating plums and raisins and drinking so much after supper." July 23, "For eating so many plums, although thou heard that many died of surfeits." August 6, "My longing after damsons when I made my vow not to eat in the orchard." August 13, "My intemperate eating of damsons, also my intemperate eating of cheese after supper." August 21, "My long sleeping in the morning."

As an eater of damson plums and cheese he may endear himself to many of us, as well as for his sluggish hearing of sermons. This young would-be divine was human and loving, without any really mortal sins. Of him one said, "He was a Moses not only for slowness of speech [he stuttered] but otherwise meekness of nature."

At the time he began work on the Bible, he sadly told himself in his diary: "Remember, on Wednesday January 18th was the day when the surplice was first urged by the archbishop to be brought into Emmanuel College. God grant that worse things do not follow the so strict urging of this indifferent ceremony. Alas, we little expected that King James would have been the first permitter of it to be brought into our college to make us a derision to so many that bear us no good will." Doddridge said of Samuel Ward, "His language is generally proper, elegant, and nervous," with a mixture of fancy in his writings.

From him we get glimpses of the unsure status of many of the clergy. They were often shaken men amid shaking forces. The Bible task was solid, while the churches swayed with fears as the winds of clashing doctrines swept around them.

The vigor and daring that young Samuel Ward lacked, Andrew Downes possessed. He appears to have been the only one of the learned men who got any money out of King James. He was born about 1549, and went to grammar school in Shrewsbury. At St. John's College, Cambridge, Downes was distinguished for his Greek scholarship. One who heard his lectures on Demosthenes said that he was ushered into the presence of a tall, long-faced, elderly person with ruddy complexion and bright eyes, who sat with his legs on the table. Downes at once gave his long, learned talk without stirring his feet or body. He was one of the few who quarreled with his fellows. He was sure of himself.

John Bois (or Boys) was in some ways the most vivid of the translators. At any rate we have more about his private life and his ways of doing than we have of others. His grandfather, also John, was a clothier of Halifax, Yorkshire. The son, William, father of our John, was born and brought up there, studied music and surgery, went to Cambridge, and thought of the Church until he broke with Rome. Then he settled on a farm at Nettlestead near Hadley; until, on joining the Church of England, he became rector at West Stow. He married Mirabel Pooley.

John Bois the translator was born January 3, 1560. His father taught him Hebrew when he was five years old. Later, John walked four miles a day to school at Hadley, where he knew John Overall, the future Dean of St. Paul's, and likewise a translator. At length he went to St. John's College, Cambridge, where Andrew Downes, the chief lecturer in Greek, read to his students twelve of the hardest Greek authors.

When Bois was chosen a fellow of Magdalene, he was lying ill of smallpox. Because Downes was careful for the new fellow's seniority, he had Bois carried on his sickbed, wrapped in blankets, to be entered. Bois had meant to study physic and had bought many books "in that faculty." He went to the university library at four in the morning and stayed until eight at night without any breaks. In reading the books on physic, "He was conceited that whatsoever disease he read of, he was troubled with the same himself. By which sickness of the brain it pleased God to cure the church of the want of so good a member as he afterwards proved." For ten years Bois was chief Greek lecturer in the college, reading his lecture in his chamber at four in the morning to many fellows and others.

He succeeded his father as rector at West Stow in 1591, but resigned that living when his mother went to live with her brother Pooley. Up to this time John seems to have been his mother's boy, married to his thoughts, but romance was thrust upon him. A Mr. Holt, rector of Boxworth near Cambridge, when about to die left the advowson, or right of presentation, to that living "in part of a portion" to one of his daughters. He asked some of his friends that, "if it might be by them procured," Bois "might become his successor by the marriage of his daughter." Bois went to look her over and soon after, "they taking liking each of the other," he received the living, and was "instituted by my lord's grace of Canterbury," who was then Whitgift. The marriage often vexed his spirit, but at thirty-six Bois was old enough to know his own mind.

Before he was married, "that he might be as well clear of the suspicion as the fault of having a wife and a fellowship at once, he desired three fellows of his own college to publish the banns on matrimony on three Sundays in his own parish church." The college, when he had to resign as fellow, gave him a hundred pounds.

Though for some years he had a rupture, Bois was robust. An early biographer described him as having an "able, active body for walking, riding, and, in his youth, for swimming." Often he walked out of his college in the morning to dine with his mother in Suffolk twenty miles away. While walking he took a book to read, if he fell into company he liked not. On horseback he used by the way to meditate on doubts, wherein he might, propounding them, require satisfaction of his learned friends in Cambridge. There is a legend, too, that he did some of the Bible work on horseback. Amid all this study he found time to beget four sons and two daughters.

When he began to know his neighbors in the country, they met Friday afternoons to discuss and resolve their scholarly doubts. As a husband and father, he kept some young scholar in his house as well for the teaching of his own children and the poorer sorts of the town people, also "because many knights and gentlemen of quality did importune him to take their children to board with him and to take some care in their training, as well for learning as manners." Thus Bois was the only translator who took in boarders.

"But as by this means the scale of his living was sunk daily lower by the greatness of the weight, so that of his estate was by the emptiness become a very unequal counterpoise. For he, minding nothing but his book, and his wife, through want of age and experience, not being able sufficiently to manage things aright, he was, ere he was aware, fallen into debt. The weight whereof (though it was not great) when he began to feel, he forthwith parted with his darling (I mean his library) which he sold (considering what it cost him) I believe to nigh as much loss as his debt amounted to, for the discharge whereof he sold it."

Never able to keep his wife subject to him, as Francis Dillingham had advised, perhaps he thought often of Paul's letter to Timothy: "Let the woman learn in silence with all subjection." Paul also declared that if a woman will learn anything, let her ask her husband at home. Clearly Mrs. Bois was a thorn in her husband's flesh.

"There grew some discontent betwixt him and his wife, insomuch that I have heard (but never from himself) that he did once intend to travel beyond the seas. But religion and conscience soon gave those thoughts the check, and made it be with him and his wife as chirurgeons say it's with a broken bone: if once well set, the stronger for a fracture." So after this strain or fracture he went on letting his wife handle the money as before.

A most exact grammarian, Bois had read sixty grammars. He had only two meals, dinner and supper, betwixt which he never so much as drank, unless, upon trouble with wind, some small quantity of acqua vitae (brandy?) and sugar. After meat he was careful almost to curiosity in picking and rubbing his teeth, esteeming that a special preservative to health, by which means he carried to his grave almost a Hebrew alphabet of teeth. Then he used to sit or walk an hour or more to digest his meat before he would go to his study. He fasted sometimes twice a week, or once in three weeks. Later he never studied between supper and bed, but spent two hours at least with friends, hearing and telling harmless delightful stories whereof he was exceedingly full. He studied standing, except when he eased himself upon his knees; but he never studied in the draft from a window, and never went to bed with cold feet.

Respectful of superiors, he was loving of equals, familiar with inferiors, though humility made him think not many below himself. He gave and forgave, being hospitable to strangers, real to friends, a just keeper of his promises. Prudently he refrained from meddling in other men's matters. A most careful, affectionate father, if displeased he denied the children his blessing morning and evening when they requested it, sometimes on two days for reasons best known to himself. As a most loving husband he had suffered, but he still committed the whole government of the house to his wife, never encroaching upon the woman's part in economic discipline.

In his piety he always knelt with his family on bare bricks. Often he prayed while he was walking, for he

[67]

approved of frequent, rather long prayers. A most diligent, attentive hearer of sermons, he endeavored when he preached to be rightly understood even of his meanest auditors.

There we have a sketch of a devout Bible-maker, with his virtues and his crotchets, his wind and his firmness, his liking for details, and his reserves of strength. Through all his household straits, about his wife, about money, about all sorts of junctures, he prepared himself to forward the Bible in English, for the Bible takes up those troubles and affords comfort to the distraught. These learned men were more than aloof, cloistered saints. Though versed in tongues, they were also just folks.

The six groups formed a kind of loose congress or council, meeting in the three places, Westminster, Oxford, and Cambridge. All were staunchly against the papists, but being all against something is not enough to unite people; they must unite in being for something real to them. These learned men were for a fresh Bible, and as scholars they were also for Hebrew, Greek, and English, for a working union of tongues. Sometimes jealous of each other, in the manner of scholars at all times, they kept their conflicts subject to their basic aims, which were broadly at one. And though they brought to the project varied points of view, they ultimately had to choose.

# CHAPTER 7

# Starting the Work

The translators went to work with zeal and forethought, here slowly and there fast. Edward Lively at Cambridge was an organizer and planner on whom all the Hebrew group there, and others too, could depend. Lancelot Andrewes, Dean of Westminster, was ardent and busy. These two were foremost among the directors.

John Overall, the prosy Dean of St. Paul's who had a wife on whom he must keep an eye; Hadrian Saravia, the most strict of the high churchmen; Laurence Chaderton, the grave Puritan, and John Rainolds, the Puritan father of the King James Bible; William Barlow, Dean of Chester, who wrote of the Hampton Court meeting, and Miles Smith who saw the work through from first to last; John Layfield who had been to the New World; Richard Thomson the Arminian who drank his fill daily; Francis Dillingham who knew what a wife should be though he never had one; stern Thomas Ravis the Dean of Christ Church; handsome plump Sir Henry Savile whom his students disliked; George Abbot the dull plodder who rose beyond all the others because his mother caught and ate a pike, and Samuel Ward the Puritan sinner with remorse of conscience; Andrew Downes who was forthright and full of vigor but jealous; and John Bois the man of all work who has shown us how they all conferred— these were among the translators who stood out.

Yet we must suspect that many of the rest, about whom we know too little, may have given much to the King James version as it stands. They were weavers of a tough, pliant fabric, full of figures, conceits, and subtle shadings, which had to withstand the wear and tear of ages. Each insight counted. The abstract and the concrete had to blend in the one immense design.

When the three groups met at their respective centers, they had a set of guiding principles which Bishop Bancroft, with advice from others, had prepared or at least approved. We must credit the valiant, ambitious Bancroft with being able to choose and manage firmly. All looked up to him, even those who deplored him and winced at his methods. He doubtless consulted a good deal with Dr. Andrewes, described as sweet and smiling, who was directly under him to handle details.

The rules which the powers of Church and state composed were as follows:

1. The ordinary Bible read in church, commonly called the Bishops' Bible, to be followed and as little altered as the truth of the original will permit.
2. The names of the prophets and the holy writers with the other names of the text to be retained as nigh as may be, accordingly as they were vulgarly used.
3. The old ecclesiastical words to be kept, viz. the word "church" not to be translated "congregation." (The Greek word can be translated either way.)
4. When a word hath divers significations, that to be kept which hath been most commonly used by most of the ancient fathers.
5. The division of the chapters to be altered either not at all or as little as may be.
6. No marginal notes at all to be affixed, but only for the explanation of the Hebrew or Greek words, which cannot without some circumlocution be so briefly and fitly expressed in the text.
7. Such quotations of places to be marginally set down as

shall serve for the fit reference of one scripture to another.

8. Every particular man of each company to take the same chapter or chapters, and having translated or amended them severally by himself, where he thinketh good, all to meet together to confer when they have done, and agree for their parts what shall stand.

9. As any one company hath dispatched any one book in this manner they shall send it to the rest, to be considered of seriously and judiciously, for His Majesty is very careful in this point.

10. If any company upon the review of the book so sent doubt or differ upon any place, to send them word thereof with the place, and withal send the reasons; to which if they consent not, the difference to be compounded at the general meeting which is to be of the chief persons of each company at the end of the work. (Thus in the end they all had to agree enough to let all readings pass.)

11. When any place of special obscurity be doubted of, letters to be directed by authority to send to any learned man in the land for his judgment of such a place.

12. Letters to be sent from every bishop to the rest of his clergy, admonishing them of his translation in hand, and to move and charge as many as being skillful in the tongues and having taken pains in that way, to send his particular observations to the company, either at Westminster, Cambridge, or Oxford. (This indicates that many must have aided in the work.)

13. The directors of each company to be the deans of Westminster and Chester for that place, and the King's professors in the Hebrew or Greek in either university.

14. These translations to be used when they agree better with the text than the Bishops' Bible—Tyndale's, Matthew's, Coverdale's, Whitchurch's (Great Bible), Geneva.

15. Besides the said directors before mentioned, three or four of the most ancient and grave divines in either of the universities, not employed in translating, to be assigned by the vice-chancellor, upon conference with the rest of the heads, to be overseers of the translation, as well Hebrew as Greek, for the better observation of the fourth rule above specified.

Some historians have said that nothing came of the plan for overseers. But a letter, dated April 19, 1605, from Thomas Bilson, Bishop of Winchester, to Sir Thomas Lake, secretary to the king, refers to Dr. George Ryves, "warden of New College in Oxford and one of the overseers of that part of the New Testament that is being translated out of Greek." The king had said, as we have seen, that any vacant living worth more than twenty pounds a year should be reserved for a translator. Bishop Bilson, himself one of those who reviewed the translators' work and made final revisions, asked the king to permit Ryves and Nicholas Love, schoolmaster of Winchester, to exchange some livings within Bilson's gift, "So that they may lay more together." This implies that both Ryves and Love, though not of the translators, had a clearly defined assignment. "The men," Bilson said, "are both of good report, the one employed in the oversight of the translation, and the other takes no small pains in doing his duty." George Ryves, born in 1569, was a son of John Ryves of Damory Court, near Blandford, Dorset, and Elizabeth, daughter of Sir John Merwyn of Fonthill, Wiltshire. He had been Warden, or head, of New College since 1599. In his mid-thirties, he was hardly one of the "most ancient" divines, though ancient had a wide meaning. Perhaps his work on the Bible was partly going from one learned man to another, to keep them informed of the work of their associates and to prod them.

Other writers have stressed that the work was slow in starting. On this point there is a letter of Lancelot Andrewes, dated the last of November, 1604, to a Mr. Hartwell: "But that this afternoon is our translation time, and most of our company are negligent, I would have seen you; but no translation shall hinder me, if once I may understand I shall commit no error in coming." Thus we see that the work at Westminster began promptly, though some of the Hebrew group there were unprepared or had stayed away when they should have met and discussed.

Understandable delay, as in many literary undertakings, must have occurred when other duties intervened because, as we have seen, translation was a part-time job without regular pay. Yet aside from providing them with fixed fees or salaries, the king was as good as his word in aiding the select divines. To Edward Lively, the royal "Hebrew reader at Cambridge," who, having lost his wife, had eleven children left out of thirteen, he gave, September 10, 1604, the living at Purleigh, Essex, a few miles from Cambridge. A month later he urged that Thomas Ravis, Dean of Christ Church, be Bishop of Gloucester. In 1605 there was a decree of the chapter at York to keep a residentiary's place for Andrew Bing. He was subdean of York for forty-six years.

William Barlow, Dean of Chester, in 1605 also, rose a little to be Bishop of Rochester. As Rochester was the least, the poorest, of the dioceses, he chose for his seal, with forlorn, brave meekness, a Latin motto which meant "set down in the lowest room." That year too the good Lancelot Andrewes, who had refused Queen Elizabeth's offer to make him a bishop, became Bishop of Chichester, southwest of London. Later Andrewes became the king's almoner, and received a grant to retain his place as prebend of St. Paul's and all his emoluments until October 2, 1607, on account of the poverty of his Chichester bishopric. Thus did the king reward his preferred translator.

On July 12, 1605, Bancroft made Jeffrey King vicar of Horsham, Sussex. The Earl of Exeter on August 19 wrote to Salisbury (Cecil) asking that his chaplain, Dr. John Layfield, who had some years since returned from his voyage of romance to the West Indies, be made parson at Gravely.

There were other cases in which, after appeals and wangling by the mighty and lesser folk, learned men rose a bit in the complex, sacred scales of the Church and received rewards for added duties, without direct grants from the king. Yet the extra appointment entailed additional duties which had nothing to do with the work of translation. On November 1, 1606, Sir Henry Savile, the plump translator who was the unpopular Master of Merton College, wrote to Sir Thomas Lake a plaintive letter which showed how many other matters a translator might have to keep in mind. "I have sent the bearer my man," he wrote, "to understand whether you have moved His Majesty for some timber trees for his poor and ancient college of Merton, Oxford. The work will be great and cost £3000; 300 trees will not furnish us . . . but I dare not present a petition for more than 100 which I hope will not be denied."

Besides the interruption of outside labors, the learned men had also, almost from the beginning, the interruption of death. Dr. Richard Edes, Dean of Worcester, died November 19, 1604, perhaps before he could do any work on the Bible, though he may have left some notes of use to his colleagues.

Then to the dismay of all concerned, Edward Lively, one of the chairmen to whom the divines and scholars were to send their advice, took sick with "an ague and a squinsey," died in four days, and was buried at St. Edward's, Cambridge, May 7, 1605, only seven months after he had received the good living at Purleigh, Essex. It was said that "too earnest study and pains about the translation hastened his death." Though he left eleven orphans without means of support, they survived and did well, and there are descendants of Edward Lively in the United States today. There is a statement that his death delayed the others who had begun to amend the Scriptures, yet they took the loss in their stride and went forward.

Early in the year 1606 died Ralph Hutchinson, the Westminster translator, aged about fifty-seven. He left a few notes about phrases in the New Testament. John Bois used these, which still exist in copy. They show how early the most painful re-examination of the Bible text began, and how the final product came from joint efforts.

Others replaced those who died, but who replaced whom? The accounts are clouded and conflicting. One replacement was Dr. John Aglionby, born about 1566, fellow of Queen's College, Oxford, a chaplain to Queen Elizabeth, principal in 1601 of Edmund Hall, Oxford, and a chaplain to King James as soon as he came to the throne. Punning on his name, they compared him to an eagle—"He was of an aquiline acumen." Then there was Leonard Hutton, who was born about 1557, received his early training at the Westminster school, was a student at St. John's College, Oxford, and was vicar of Floore, Northamptonshire, in 1601. In 1592 for Queen Elizabeth's visit to Oxford he wrote a play in Latin about a war of grammar between two rival kings, verb and noun. His Latin verses are to be found today at Oxford. He became subdean of Christ Church, and after Robert Burton settled there, the two must have known each other well. In 1600 Hutton engaged in a solemn disputation, worthy of Burton, about whether in the rebirth concupiscence is a sin. He married Anne Hamden, and had a daughter, Alice.

So far we have met forty-seven translators out of the king's original fifty-four, all that are named on the chief lists that have come down to us. To these should be added the name of William Thorne, for whom there is ample evidence.

In 1606 fourteen bishops, among them Bilson of Winchester and Ravis of Gloucester, both translators, signed with many a flourish a formal plea: "At the request of Doctor Thorne, his majesty's chaplain, we whose names are hereunto subscribed have thought it equal and just to make known unto all, whom it appertaineth, that he hath for many years read the public Hebrew lecture with very good recommendation in the University of Oxford, that he is now likewise very necessarily employed in the translation of that part of the Old Testament which is remitted to that university, that he doth govern in the church of Chichester where he is dean with judgment and discretion, and that in the one and the other place he hath ever been and now is of very good and honest reputation. In regard whereof our opinion and hope is that he will approve himself worthy of further promotion in the church." Despite the lofty commendation, Thorne failed to be preferred much more, but he earned the name of translator.

Additional names of which mention may be found besides those of Leonard Hutton, John Aglionby, and Thomas Bilson, already referred to, were Daniel Featley, born Fairclough, Arthur Lake, James Montague, who became Bishop of Bath and Wells, Thomas Sparke who had been at Hampton Court but is mentioned as a translator only in a life of King James on which one can hardly depend, and William Eyre. Some authorities say that Daniel Featley was too young to share in the work; others that he had something to do with it, and he is on the British Museum list of translators. Perhaps many of these names are false leads. Proof, one way or the other, is most difficult. The surmise that many aided in the translation unofficially, seems justified. Many must have offered advice on verses, helped solve hard problems, and queried readings on which the chosen learned men agreed. Hugh Broughton, the rabid Puritan, was angry at being left out, but his friends among the translators may have consulted him and used some of his phrasings.

The lives of the learned men were quiet, except for their many mundane duties. Years later John Selden wrote in his *Table Talk*, "The translation in King James' time took an excellent way. That part of the Bible was given to him who was most excellent in such a tongue (as the Apocrypha to Andrew Downes) and then they met together, and one read that translation, the rest holding in their hands some Bible, either of the learned tongues, or French, Italian, Spanish &c. If they found any fault, they spoke; if not, he read on." Andrew Downes dealt with many other books than those of the Apocrypha, for he was learned in the Greek of the New Testament too.

What ancient-language texts did they work with? They had the Complutensian Polyglot of 1517, published at Complutus, now Alcara de Henares, Spain, and they had the Antwerp Polyglot, 1569–72. These gave Hebrew and Greek texts with versions in other tongues added. Of course they had the Latin Vulgate, though that was suspect because it was popish. With some fragments of early scrolls, they had countless comments by the early church fathers and ancient scholars. Often they referred to St. Chrysostom (347–407 A.D.), whose works Sir Henry Savile had begun to edit, with help from Andrew Downes and John Bois. Another reference authority was the Geneva scholar, Theodore Beza (1519–1605).

Since the time of King James other Bible manuscripts and fragments have come to light, though none, save perhaps the Isaiah of the Dead Sea Scrolls, goes back to early Christian days, let alone to its original writer. The various manuscripts and fragments contain thousands of variant readings, throughout. What the King James men had, and what we have today in greater variety, consists of copies derived from former copies and so on backward. The text as it stands in any scholarly edition must, by the very nature of the problem, be in many respects corrupt. We can only trust that what we have is a reasonably accurate text of the sixty-six books, which through the ages the churches came to accept as the Holy Scriptures. It should be obvious, therefore, that no English rendition is, or can be from any literary standpoint, the precise word of God.

[ 77 ]

# CHAPTER 8

# King's Pleasure

While the scholars were busy with the Bible, their royal patron was pursuing his usual interests. Twice a week at Whitehall there were cockfights, and in November of 1604 the king was much at Royston.

Royal visits were an expense hard to be borne by the countryside so honored. One day a favorite among the king's hounds, Howler, was missing. The next day in the field Howler came in among the rest of the hounds. The king, glad of his return, spied a paper about his neck: "Good Mr. Howler, we pray you speak to the King (for he hears you every day and so doth he not us) that it will please His Majesty to go back to London, for else the country will be undone; all our provision is spent already, and we are not able to entertain him longer." Unperturbed by this plain speaking from the local farmers who had to supply his retinue, King James stayed on for a fortnight.

On December 4 the Earl of Worcester wrote from Royston, "In the morning we are on horseback by eight, and so continue in full career from the death of one hare to another until four at night . . . five miles from home."

All this was while Bancroft was taking office as Archbishop, and Lancelot Andrewes was faithfully setting aside his days for "translation time."

At the Christmas season, 1604, Sir Philip Herbert married Lady Susan Vere in the king's presence. The bride and groom lodged in the council chamber at White-hall, where the king in shirt and nightgown conducted a reveille matin before they were up, even lolling on the bed. In such coarse doings James behaved as if the Bible had no effect on him. Yet he continued to show interest in the new translation and in time gave preferment to the translators one by one.

The day before Twelfth Night, James made young Prince Charles Duke of York. For Twelfth Night there was Ben Jonson's *Masque of Blackness.* The queen was six months pregnant, but again she and her ladies, this time with blackened faces and arms, appeared in the play with their hair down and wore rich gauzy draperies which shocked the guests. Courtiers in the masque were dressed as Moors, riding sea horses and other frightful fishes. At the banquet, guests so wildly assailed the king's provisions that tables and trestles went down before any could touch the food, and jewels and gold chains were lost in the scramble. The king joined in the gaming after-wards.

Such royal routs cost thousands of pounds. The learned men who revised the Scriptures were, meanwhile, getting nothing except their rooms and commons while they were away from home. Weekly they returned on horseback or afoot to their churches where they had to conduct many a service. At the New Year those of them who were bishops sent the king from ten to thirty pounds in gold.

On February 8 there was a play, *The Fair Maid of Bristol,* at Whitehall. Two weeks later the king went to Newmarket, which was starting its long sporting career in horse racing.

For the queen's lying-in there was much clamor about who should carry the white staff, hold the back of the chair, keep the door, rock the cradle, and such services, all more or less fixed by custom. The birth of the princess was on April 8. She lived only a little over two years.

[ 79 ]

Continuing their royal revels, on June 3 the king and his party went again to the Lion's Tower. There they watched live cocks thrown to male and female lions and torn to pieces. But when the keeper lowered a live lamb into the cage, the lions merely sniffed at it and let it alone. Alas, the lions had no real chance to lie down with the lamb, for at this point the keepers lifted it out safely.

Presumably the work of translation continued peaceably amid the court activities in sports, gaming, and amateur theatricals, but during the next year one royal pastime inevitably disturbed the translators. This was the visit of King James to Oxford, August 27, 1605. Corpus Christi College has preserved the charge to heads of houses over a month before this royal progress:

1. All doctors and graduates, scholars, fellows and probationers to provide before the first day of August next gowns, hood, and cape according to the statutes of their houses and orders of the university, and that all commoners and halliers do wear round caps, and colors and fashions in their apparel as the statutes do provide.
2. That whosoever shall be seen by the vice chancellor or protectors or other overseers appointed by the delegates in the street or any public place, during the King's Majesty's abode, otherwise apparelled than the statutes of their houses or the university appoint for their degree, shall presently forfeit ten pounds and suffer imprisonment at the discretion of the said officers, the said forfeit to be levied by the vice chancellor or whom he shall appoint.
3. That upon the day when the King cometh, all graduates shall be ready at the ringing of St. Maries bell to come in their habits and hoods according to their degrees, and all scholars in their gowns and caps shall stand quietly in such order as shall be appointed, until his majesty be passed into Christ Church, and the train being passed, every one may report to his own college.
4. That all scholars, bachelors, and masters do diligently fre-

quent the ordinary lectures during the time of his majesty's abode.

5. That no scholar of what degree soever presume to come upon the state in St. Maries, upon pain of one month's imprisonment and forty pounds fine, and that no master of arts presume to come within the compass of the rail or stage below, where the disputers sit, but with his hood turned according to his degree, and none but masters of arts and bachelors of law shall presume to come into that place.

6. That the scholars which cannot be admitted to see the plays do not make any outcries or undecent noise about the hall, stairs, or within the quadrangle of Christ Church, upon pain of present imprisonment and any other punishment according to the direction of the vice chancellor and proctors.

7. That they warn their companies to provide verses to be disposed and set upon St. Maries, or to other places convenient, and that those verses be corrected by the deans or some others appointed by the head.

8. That a short oration be provided at every house to entertain his majesty if his pleasure be to visit the same, and verses set up.

9. That University College, All Souls, and Magdalen College do set up verses at his majesty's departure, upon such places so as they may be seen as he passeth by.

10. That the fellows and scholars of the body of each house be called home and not permitted to go abroad till after his majesty be gone from the university, and that they may be at home by the first of August.

The vice-chancellor in charge of all this was Dr. George Abbot, the translator for whom the future promised so much. As acting head of Oxford he was to collect the fines, see that there was a full turnout in fancy dress, and make sure that no wicked students—most of them teen-aged, like college boys today—spoiled the solemn display. He had a month to prepare, and many of the Oxford translators who would otherwise have used the summer months for study of the Bible texts must have had to help him.

[*81*]

For the king's visit Oxford paved streets and swept them well. It newly painted all rails, posts, bars of windows, casements, and pumps, and newly tricked all arms. On August 27 the king came riding horseback, with the queen on his left hand, Prince Henry before them. Because they had come by easy stages, stopping nights at great houses, they were fresh enough to look regal. The vice-chancellor, George Abbot, translator, made his speech on his knee with good grace and a clear voice.

The party went on to St. John's College. At Carfax Dr. John Perin, Greek reader and a translator, made his oration "in good familiar Greek." The king heard him willingly and the queen gladly, because she said she had never heard Greek. Dry as such a program may seem to us today, to the scholars, and even to the royal group, such speeches were alive and of intense concern, partly because they all looked with respect on heaven and hell. Who was good enough to regard the future with peace of mind?

The party progressed to Christ Church, and on the second day, August 28, from ten in the morning until one they watched a tiresome light play. But the sermons, lectures, disputes, and speeches of the translators and the rest went on and on in accord with the schedule. The Latin verses by the students, gone over by the deans, were all up in place. Here and there the gracious king, twiddling his fingers as was his wont, gave a few words of praise, often in Latin. Vice-chancellor Abbot sent Dr. Aglionby around with the king, whose alert vigor amazed all. There is no suggestion that he drank too much. This was a fair of learning on a high plane, with even the youthful scholars less noisy and rowdy than was their habit, and the doctors of divinity arrayed in scarlet gowns, faced down to the feet with velvet, in the hot August weather.

That summer appeared the first catalogue of the new Oxford library to which the year before King James had, by patent, given the name of its founder, Sir Thomas Bodley. It listed among the thousands of books in its 655 pages, *Biblia Latina pulcherrima*, two volumes, a present from Dr. George Ryves, Warden of New College and an overseer of the translation, and other books that were gifts from the King James learned men. Today the Bodleian has hundreds of papers, as well as books, by and about the translators.

Though his life belied it, King James seemed sincere enough in posing as a lover of books. When he received his degree at Oxford, he went into the Bodleian, where chains bound all the books to the shelves. Looking around with a longing mien, he said, "I would wish, if ever it be my lot to be carried captive, to be shut up in this prison, to be bound with these chains, and to spend my life with these fellow captives which stand here chained." James truly admired the Bodleian.

Today it may be asked whether the learned men of Oxford admired the king. Now he was the guest of some who had been his guests at Hampton Court; Dr. John Rainolds was one, on a program of sermons and lectures in Latin and English. Although Rainolds' lecture [1] has not been preserved, it seems safe to assume that he was more polite to his king than James, at the conference, had been to him.

In fact Rainolds the Puritan was finding it possible to conform to some of the most difficult of the church claims. In a letter dated June 3, 1605, two months before the king's visit, he maintained that the bishops and clergy since Henry VIII's split with the Roman Church had been rightly ordained, and even in some cases confirmed by the Pope. Many chief doctors of the Roman Church had taught, he said, "Out of St. Augustine, grounding on the

---

[1] A "sermon" was delivered within the church service; a "lecture" outside it, even though in the church building. New England later kept up the custom of lecture day in the meeting house.

Scripture that heretical bishops may lawfully ordain." Therefore in this letter, still among the Corpus Christi papers, Rainolds joined Bancroft and the king in arguing that the Church of England had wholly correct descent from St. Peter, and its clergy were in the direct, sacred line from the first Christian bishops.

Rainolds made no mention at this time of the divine right of kings, but years before, in another letter, he had written about divinity. "Sith that divinity, the knowledge of God, is the water of life, the vessel must be cleansed that shall have God's holy spirit not only a guest but also a continual dweller within. God forbid that you should think divinity consists of words, as a wood doth of trees. Divinity without godliness doth but condemn consciences against the day of vengeance, and provide the wrath of the mighty Lord, and make more inexcusable before the seat of judgment. . . . True divinity cannot be learned unless we frame our hearts and minds wholly to it." He had then urged study of the word of God in the Hebrew and Greek, "not out of the books of translation," and had approved strongly of painful travail in Calvin's works. Now, still for Calvin, he was also for the translation that was James's best claim to divine guidance.

And indeed the Bible men were for the king, the master of their task. Though the King James version as it came from their hands and minds contained much against kings, preachers could and did conclude that it stood for divine right of the crown. Among the translators, Lancelot Andrewes, whom the king heard preach and greatly approved, said: "The duties of a king are first to acknowledge his power to be from God. . . . Another duty of the people is to bear with the infirmities of this mild king, and to be as meek toward him in covering his uncomeliness, if any be." Was James thus mild and meek? Or was Andrewes just holding up before him a standard?

In another sermon the gentle Andrewes uttered what

we may now see as a warning, though surely it was not so meant or understood. Of kings he said: "If religion make them not, heresy will not unmake them." Yet the struggles of James and the House of Commons over taxes and other matters going on around the learned men as they worked, could only confirm their religious convictions and make them the more eager to finish their special task. Let other writers—as for instance Pericles in Shakespeare—raise political issues

> Kings are earth's gods; in vice their law's their will,
> And if Jove stray, who dares say, Jove doth ill?

A touchy king might well dislike such questions, and for the progress of the Bible work it was little enough to assure a royal patron of his virtue and safety. In the long run a bright, pure Bible could help all men to stand equal before the mercy seat of heaven.

Another rebel in attendance during the royal visit was Dr. Thomas Holland, the translator who had conformed in outward things though he remained inwardly against the bishops. As a feature of the royal entertainment, Dr. Holland took part in an argument on the theological question, Do the saints and angels know the thoughts of the heart? Though an appropriate choice for men of many minds, all on their good behavior, the virtue of the question was that no one could answer it. It was therefore a perfect subject for a heated debate, a drill in what passed for logic, in the manner of the schoolmen of the Middle Ages. According to custom, Dr. John Aglionby, a translator, upheld one side and three other translators— Drs. Holland, Giles Thomson, and John Harding—argued in opposition. The moderator was to be Thomas Bilson, Bishop of Winchester, another translator, if he could come; if not, then the vice-chancellor—George Abbot, a translator too—would take his place.

Although some may have enjoyed their roles in the

celebration, for Dr. Rainolds, prime mover in a more important project, the days of the royal visit must have been an ordeal. He had long been less than robust. Coughing more than he liked, he suffered from what he and the doctors thought was gout. Rainolds aroused himself to lecture before the king, being present at all the stodgy pomps, wearing the heavy emblems of his learning, and then went back to his Corpus Christi duties and his study, where he took extreme pains in poring over the Bible sources and choosing English phrases. Normally the translators met in his quarters once a week to discuss the Bible work now put aside.

When the king left, his party and the divines, plump and lean, with all sorts of other people crowded the highways. Men, women, and children rode in a jingling traffic of gay colors. Sedate translators returned to their livings. In the stream many were walking, and there were carts for luggage and varied goods. Traffic converged on Oxford too, turning out and waiting as advance riders warned that the royal progress was coming. On the face of England there had been few changes since the time of Chaucer's pilgrims. The real changes would come when readers of the new Bible learned to overturn what James thought and urged, and to read into his Bible what he most strongly opposed.

CHAPTER 9

# Holy War

After long delays, Parliament was to meet on November 5, 1605. Great Britain still observes that date with bonfires, and boys dressing up, putting on masks, going around begging for pennies, and shouting a ragged little rhyme. On that day all who approached Whitehall and the old palace of Westminster found the streets barred by soldiers. London seethed with alarm, awe, and rumors, ill-founded and well-founded. When it appeared that Parliament was to convene still later, the crowd at length dispersed.

The trouble had begun long before. From Brussels, March 17, 1604, a newsletter had said: "It is also reported that all Catholics are to leave England on pain of death. Should anyone of this religion be met with in the future, all his property and fortune are to go to his nearest friend. It is a subtle scheme for one friend to denounce the other, wherefrom it is to be gathered what is to be expected from this king."

In secret, it is now supposed, Queen Anne had become a papist. She and the king were oddly unsure of each other, though without an open break. James meant in the main to preserve the Church of England as it was, so long as it helped preserve his kingship. Thus, angry at a report that he had become a convert of Rome, James was putting in force with doubled vigor the revived penal laws against the papists. Those who belonged to the Roman Church, many with famous old names, were enraged or in despair.

A band of them, mainly kinsfolk, had begun to plot some six months before, about the time a cuckoo flew over the pulpit of Paul's Cross and cried out—this at the time was seen as an omen of something dire to come. The story is too involved to give in detail here, but on October 26, the Lord Chamberlain, Monteagle, received an unsigned letter begging him to stay away from Parliament on the day it opened. He took the letter to Robert Cecil, who on November 1 showed it to the king at a midnight meeting. The king shrewdly surmised a good deal of what it meant.

Monday, November 4, an agent of the royal party found in a cellar beneath the House of Lords a man, named Guy Fawkes, disguised as a servant, beside piles of faggots, billets of wood, and masses of coal. The agent went away. Shortly Monteagle and one other came and talked, but gave no heed to Fawkes, who was still on guard, until they were about to go. He told them he was a servant of Thomas Percy, a well-known papist. Still later, at midnight, soldiers found Fawkes booted and spurred and with a lantern outside the cellar door. He had taken few pains to conceal his actions. They dragged him into an alley, searched him, and found on him a tinderbox and a length of slow match. In a fury now they moved the faggots, billets, and coal, and came upon barrel after barrel of powder, thirty-six barrels in all. Fawkes then confessed that he meant to blow up the House of Lords and the king.

On November 6, Percy, with others, rushed into an inn at Dunchurch, Warwickshire, with the news that the court was aware of their plan. By the eighth the whole attempt had clearly failed. When Parliament met a week after the stated day, the king, calm, gracious, and splendid, told what had happened and then adjourned the meeting.

At first Fawkes refused to name any except Percy, who, with others, was killed in the course of a chase. In time he gave the names of all, who would have blown up the House of Lords "at a clap."

Guy Fawkes was baptized at St. Michael le Belfrey, York, April 16, 1570, son of Edward Fawkes, a proctor and advocate in the church courts of York. The father died and the mother married a papist. In 1603 Guy Fawkes went to Madrid to urge that Philip III invade England. Thus he was a confirmed traitor, though egged on and used by more astute plotters.

Some of these men had been involved in the rising of the Earl of Essex. A number were former members of the Church of England. Most of them had some land and wealth. They were all highly disturbed beings, throwbacks, who meant to subvert the state and get rid of King James. Church and state, they were sure, must be at one, with fealty to the Pope.

In Westminster Hall, January 27, 1606, there was a trial after a fashion with no real defense. Sir Edward Coke simply outlined the case and asked some questions. For nearly a year, the plotters had been digging a tunnel from a distance, but had found the wall under the House of Lords nine feet thick. They had then got access to the cellar by renting a building. They had planned to kill the king, seize his children, stir up an open revolt with aid from Spaniards in Flanders, put Princess Elizabeth on the throne, and marry her to a papist. Though all but one, Sir Everard Digby, pleaded not guilty, the court, such as it was, condemned them all to death. That same week they were all hanged, four in St. Paul's churchyard, where John Overall, the translator, could have looked on, and four in the yard of the old palace. Among the latter was Guy Fawkes, tall, brown-haired, and with an auburn beard. He was so weak from torture that guards had to help him up to the scaffold. Percy and three others had been killed before while trying to escape, and one had died in prison.

Three months later came the trial of Henry Garnet, a Jesuit, thought to be head of the Jesuits in England. Brought up a Protestant, he knew of the plot but had shrunk in horror from it, though he left the chosen victims to their fate. The court condemned him also to die.

All this concerned the men at work on the Bible. At Garnet's hanging, May 3, in St. Paul's churchyard, John Overall, Dean of St. Paul's, took time off from his translating to be present. Very gravely and Christianly he and the Dean of Winchester urged upon Garnet "a true and lively faith to God-ward," a free and plain statement to the world of his offense; and if any further treason lay in his knowledge, he was begged to unburden his conscience and show a sorrow and detestation of it. Garnet, firm in his beliefs, desired them not to trouble him. So after the men assigned to the gruesome duty had hanged, drawn, and quartered the victim, Dean Overall returned to St. Paul's and his Bible task.

That year, 1606, Overall was also writing his convocation book of canons. This was intended to be a code for the faithful. A part of it upheld the divine right of kings. Yet, Overall argued, if any upset by force occurred and a new rule succeeded, this too in turn could plead for itself a divine right, and insist that the people obey it, thus to do their duty toward God. To touchy James this was false doctrine. So he suppressed the whole book of canons, which came out only after 1688, when James II was forced to leave the country.

The Guy Fawkes plot inspired many sermons. Of the translators, Ravis preached at Paul's Cross, Barlow at Westminster, and Andrewes at Whitehall. From then on Andrewes preached ten Guy Fawkes sermons before the king, one a year, deriving awful lessons from the horrid scheme.

William Barlow also preached at Paul's Cross on the Sunday after the plot came to light. His text was Psalm 18:50: "Great deliverance giveth He to His king, and sheweth mercy to His anointed, to David, and to his seed for evermore." Of Guy Fawkes Barlow said: "To make himself drunk with the blood of so many worthies . . . such heaps he had laid in of billets, faggots, large stones, iron crows, pickaxes, great hammer heads, besides so many barrels of gun powder . . . not manlike to kill but beastlike to . . . tear parcel meal the bodies of such personages . . . this whirling blast would have been unto our sacred king . . . as the whirlwind and fiery chariot of Elias, to have carried up his soul to heaven."

The first Guy Fawkes sermon by Lancelot Andrewes was on Psalm 118:23, 24: "This is the Lord's doing; it is marvellous in our eyes. This is the day which the Lord hath made; we will rejoice and be glad in it." He implied that God let the plotters proceed so that He could destroy them in signal fashion, to give the public a good lesson: "We have therefore well done . . . by law to provide that this day should not die, nor the memorial thereof perish, from ourselves or from our seed, but be consecrated to a perpetual memory, by a yearly acknowledgment to be made of it throughout all generations. . . ."

Other sermons following the Fawkes attempt were aimed directly at the papist party, now, naturally in even less favor. The Church of England had maintained, and maintains, that the Catholic Church is, as the term means, the church universal. That the Roman Church could be that church universal seemed absurd to such divines as the translator, the stodgy George Abbot. Yet he, like others to this day, confused oneness, the belief that there can be but one Christian Church, with places and numbers of people. Thus he wrote with righteous scorn to a papist, "What say you to the south continent, which is so huge a country that if the firm land do hold unto the pole, as it commonly is received and believed, it very near equaleth all Asia, Africa, and Europe, and what part in all that world is thoroughly discovered as yet by any Christian? . . . If we look unto the northern and colder parts of America, which are not so fit for the breeding of gold [how wrong he was about that!] . . . what huge countries be there of incomparable bigness which have nothing of Christianity in them?"

In other words, unless the Church of Rome had spread to all parts of the world, how could it claim to be the one church for all? He disdained the papist's mention of Goa, "as if it were some huge region, whereas it is but a city." As he argued, he contradicted himself, for he also wrote, "You are misinformed that the protestants do glory in their great number; they know that truth is truth, be it in more or few." The papists, with subdued fury about the new Bible, and the Church of England kept on pushing for themselves, and against each other. The translators worked on in this stormy air.

Nor was the controversy limited to the Catholic claims. In the summer of 1606 four divines preached before the king on how to reduce some Presbyterian Scots to a right feeling toward the Church of England. Among them were Andrewes and Barlow.

Meanwhile a young man in Holland was stirring up questions which long after involved Dr. Andrewes and George Abbot. Born in Essex about 1575, Bartholomew Legate had no college training, but, after being a dealer in cloth lists, he preached among the "Seekers," an offshoot of the Mennonites in Zeeland. He soon found that Mennonite tenet, that our Lord's body came from heaven, an "execrable heresy." By 1605 he was teaching that Jesus Christ was a mere man, but born free from sin. The Scriptures, he said, term him God, not from his essence but because of his office. This was more than any stable churchmen could endure. The case of this bold minor figure was to be as evil as that of Guy Fawkes. Tried by the London consistory, with George Abbot presiding and Lancelot Andrewes a member, Legate was condemned to death.

After the Gunpowder Plot failed, the religious conflict entered a less explosive stage, but one involving many differences of opinion. The Established Church in England, as in Rome, fought all divergences as heresy. In 1607 Thomas Ravis, the Oxford translator, became Bishop of London succeeding the man who had replaced Richard Bancroft when the latter became Archbishop of Canterbury. Ravis, always grim, at once began to harass those who would not submit fully to the Church. "By the help of Jesus," he announced with haughty sureness that Jesus was with him, "I will not leave one preacher in my diocese who doth not subscribe and conform." While he worked on the Bible, he was highly active as a hated scourge. Writing "Of Unity in Religion," Andrewes' friend Francis Bacon said, "Lukewarm persons think they may accommodate points of religion by middle ways, and taking part of both." The bishops among the translators were far from lukewarm. They had no use for middle ways.

On July 3 the king had declared: "We advise conformity especially of ministers, who have been the chief authors of divisions, and hope they will not omit substantial duties for shadows and semblance of zeal. If they are intractable, they must be compelled by the authority which we are compelled to use for preservation of the church's authority. Such as have been censured for disobedience may have till 30 November to bethink them of their course, and then either conform or dispose of themselves in other ways, as after that, proceeding will be taken against them." Though the king was competent to express himself, we may assume that he used ghost writers, among them no doubt Bancroft, Robert Cecil, and Sir Thomas Lake.

One main pinch was that all the clergy had to accept all those of the thirty-nine articles that dealt with rites and ceremonies. From a modern point of view those were the shadows, not the substance, of worship. But at the Hampton Court meeting, as we have seen, there had been controversy over making the sign of the cross, and there were many other matters in dispute.

Increasing conflict made it certain that the men added to the list of translators would be stanch supporters of the established church. This was true of Leonard Hutton, chaplain to Bishop Bancroft. At Oxford in 1605 Hutton published *An Answer to a Certain Treatise of the Cross in Baptism.* This he addressed to Richard Bancroft, Archbishop since November. In it he opposed a statement that "the sign of the cross being a human ordinance is become an idol and may not lawfully be used in the service of God." This he countered with a plea that "the consignation of a child's forehead in baptism was one of the most ancient ceremonies of Christianity." Some made a difference of the place for the sign, in baptism on the crown, in confirmation on the forehead. Many used the sign of the cross in all sorts of low ways, as on their breasts and foreheads in dice playing, to bring them luck.

Hutton went on, "How much better were it to turn these forces that are spent upon ourselves against the common adversary who (as lamentable experience hath taught us) maketh this strife of ours a fit occasion and instrument to overthrow our common faith." That urging of common sense and oneness meant, alas, that all the Puritans should accept his point of view. It never occurred to him that those who liked the cross in baptism might use it, and that those who disliked it might reject it.

"These things and many other grievous sins and works of darkness, that blush not . . . to show themselves in the open day, could not thus swarm amongst us as daily they do, if we all truly intended the same thing, if we could faithfully and unfeignedly give one another the right hand of fellowship, and seriously do the Lord's work with one consent." Again this hearty standing for that one consent meant that all should consent to what Hutton believed; stop all this silly fighting, and agree with what I tell you! He wrote further: "That which I would now say is, to desire the treatiser and his friends that they would first reform themselves." What could be more within reason? It may seem to us today that he was writing not really to persuade those on the other side of the wordy contest, but to please his master, Bancroft, head of the Church under the king.

Loving peace on his own terms, Hutton had a tranquil life, while the Puritans waxed more potent around him. "If you fear a curse," he said grandly, "you fear where no cause of fear is." A stained glass window at Christ Church bears the arms of this translator and two other Oxonians, Edes and Ravis.

As the conflicts continued, the power of the bishops, an issue at Hampton Court, became stronger. "The occasion which caused the apostles to appoint bishops," Andrewes said, "seemeth to have been schisms." Again he said, "The whole ministry of the New Testament was at the first invested in Christ alone. He is termed . . . bishop, I Peter 2:25."

Bishop Barlow preached on the antiquity and supremacy of bishops, using as his text Acts 20:28, "Take heed therefore with yourselves, and to all the flock over whom the Holy Ghost hath made you overseers, to feed the church of God, which he hath purchased with his own blood." It was clear to Barlow that overseers meant bishops. Yet to this day scholars in commentaries argue whether the Greek word rendered in English as bishop meant what we mean by bishop at all. Given the times and the number of bishops among the learned men, the new Bible was certain to sustain the cult of bishops wherever the chance arose.

Of the bishops one at least was to be highly useful. For Thomas Bilson, Bishop of Winchester, with Miles Smith, at the end revised all that the rest had done. He was one on whom the king and his trusted churchmen relied. We may well ask how his style fitted him to burnish the whole final draft, but if we use this criterion we may ask in vain. Bishop Bilson was for the most part a dull writer. So are many first-rate editors.

He was born in Winchester in 1547, the son of German parents. His father, Herman, was a son of Arnold and perhaps a daughter of a duke of Bavaria. At New College, Oxford, Thomas Bilson became a doctor of divinity in 1581, and was raised to Bishop of Winchester in 1597. In many ways he carried on the holy warfare of the Church; at New College in 1599, where the Puritans were getting stronger, he had to insist on the wearing of surplice and hood with the same firmness with which he forbade taking meat from the kitchen and bread from the buttery between meals. Liking philosophy, physics, and divinity, the bishop was also fond of poetry. In that fondness we may find a clue to his skill with the Bible work toward the end. But mainly, being very well aware of the church conflicts that had always been rampant, Bilson was correct in dogma, a safe man to steady the king's new English Bible. One said of Bishop Bilson that he "carried prelature in his very aspect."

On "the perpetual government of Christ's church," Bilson said: "The second assured sign of episcopal power is imposition of hands to ordain presbyters and bishops, for as pastors were to have some to assist them in their charge, which were presbyters, so· were they to have others to succeed them in their places which were bishops. And this right by imposing hands to ordain presbyters and bishops in the church of Christ was at first derived from the apostles unto bishops not unto presbyters."

Thus he was ready to squelch the Presbyterian nonsense which the king hated. The word "presbyters" appears only once in the King James Bible, but the Greek word thus rendered is in many other places translated "elders." The Presbyterians have survived all the would-be squelchings by Bilson and others. The good bishop himself commented on differences of opinion as inevitable:

"Who doth marvel that amongst so many thousands of bishops as the whole world yielded in so many hundred years there should be some contentious and ambitious spirits. . . . Were the pastors but of England, France, and Germany to meet in a free synod, I will not ask you when they would agree, but if their tongues be like their pens, there would be more need of officers to part the frays than of notaries to write the acts."

The Bible on which the translators worked was born amid vivid and ruthless controversy. Yet outwardly at least the learned men made their peace with authority. On December 20, 1606, Dr. John Duport, the translator who was master of Jesus College, Cambridge, declared that all of that house conformed to the doctrine and discipline of the Church of England. By then all the Puritan translators had conformed enough to escape being banished or direly punished in other ways. That month Archbishop Bancroft began to proceed against any Puritan clergy who were stubborn, and in a year, some historians say, got rid of three hundred, though others say fewer.

In 1607 a number of these men found an alternative: they sailed to Virginia. In due course the Puritans won England for a time, and then lost, while they long triumphed in America.

# CHAPTER 10

# Private Fortunes

On Eleventh and Twelfth Nights, 1606, just before the hanging of the gunpowder plotters, the *Masque of Hymen* by Ben Jonson cheered the wedding of Robert Devereux, Earl of Essex, and Lady Frances, daughter of the Earl of Suffolk. This Essex, son of the Essex who lost his head, was a boy of fourteen and his bride was a girl of thirteen. Years later two of the translators had to do something further about the marriage.

Now Lancelot Andrewes, while he translated, was in the thick of events, both gay and grave. By disposition and training it was easy for him to turn his thoughts from the divine to the secular, from the scholarly to the worldly. At Westminster he saw to the repair of the dean's lodgings, and when he went to Chichester as bishop he repaired the palace. Often he was with the king at Newmarket for the horse racing and the bloodier sports. We may surmise that his sermons served to make the king less trying.

As Bishop of Gloucester Thomas Ravis spent lavishly on social affairs, and it was said that he "in so short a time had gained the good liking of all sorts that some who could not brook the name of bishop were content to give (or rather to pay) him a good report." He also constructed conduits to bring water into his bishop's palace, built much of it anew, and improved the paving.

As the progress and advancement of the translators continued Jeffrey King, of Andrewes' Westminster Hebrew group, a fellow of King's College, became royal professor of Hebrew at Cambridge.

Bishop Barlow, the translator, had to officiate at a royal funeral. The Princess Sophia was born at Greenwich on June 22, 1606, and died the next day. A barge covered with black velvet conveyed her to the chapel royal at Westminster.

Then, in February, 1607, another translator died—William Dakins, professor of divinity at Gresham College, London.

And now the worst sling of fortune so far struck the learned men engaged on the Bible. Dr. John Rainolds, ill as he thought with the gout, had long received his fellow workers while living on a pallet in his study. On April 1, 1606, he had been sick enough to make his will. Now at last on May 21, 1607, he died, not of gout but of phthisis. "His last sickness," one said, "was contracted merely ["merely" then meant "wholly"] by exceeding pains in study by which he brought his withered body to a very skeleton." His death came only a bit over three years after the Hampton Court meeting at which he had proposed the new Bible.

His will may be seen at Corpus Christi College, to which he gave a hundred of his books. To the Bodleian he gave forty books, and to other colleges, Queen's, Merton, New, University, Oriel, Exeter, Trinity, and Brasenose, he gave many more. One of his treasures was his Regia Bible in eight volumes. There was a special bequest of books to Sir Henry Savile, his austere fellow translator, the high churchman.

To the one who would succeed him as head of Corpus Christi College he left his map of England, his linen and woolen bedding and lesser household things, and his notebooks about the college. Though we may have thought of him as a man alone, he made bequests to his two brothers and to his sister. To two friends he gave his private notebooks, papers, letters, and writings, to make away with those which could do no good, and to publish only those lectures which he had finished.

[ 99 ]

There are early letters from his friend and comrade in the translation, Ralph Hutchinson, who had died the year before. They show again how absorbed these men had always been in their Bible studies. Thus Hutchinson wrote of commentaries mentioned by one man, "The commentaries . . . I can assure you to be mere empty names. For except those which are in the Venice Bible, let any man in Christendom show me so many as he speaketh of upon the book of Esther, and I dare make myself his bondman. And even for those in the Bomberg edition of the Bible, I know not whether Ezra and Salome be joined there or no in any of those editions which are his." One problem of the learned men was to reject fakes made by pseudo scholars.

The list of Rainolds' possessions fills a long page. There were books valued at 774 pounds, 10 shillings, a large sum for those days. Maps of England, Europe, Asia, Africa, and America were worth 8 pounds, 8 shillings. His early map of America before Virginia or Plymouth was settled would be worth a good deal today.

Among his other precious things were a silver bottle, a watch, a signet, a pair of bellows, some sugar and ginger (perhaps for use in his sickness), a penknife, wax papers, and clothes. He had gowns with hoods faced with velvet, twelve pairs of stockings, a rug and a blanket, twelve fine towels, two pairs of silk garters, a muff, some gloves, and other maybe stranger objects set down in writing too difficult to read. There is no surplice on the list, though he had conformed enough to wear one. In sum they were the simple, useful goods of an eminent but quiet, devout scholar, who lived in much more comfort than Elder William Brewster and other American Pilgrim fathers some decades later. At the end of his will Rainolds gently quoted, "Give none offence, neither to the Jews, nor to the Grecians ["Gentiles" in the King James version], nor to the church of God."

Corpus Christi College chose to succeed him as president

John Spenser, a fellow translator of the Andrewes group, the preacher who had warned of how the Church as it prospers may become lax and corrupt. In the college statues the figure of Rainolds stands with a closed book, the Old Testament which he helped translate, and the figure of Spenser stands with an open book, the New Testament, on which he worked.

May 22, 1607, the day after Dr. John Rainolds died, a masque by Ben Jonson was performed before the king at Theobalds. Like other Jonson masques, it played up to James. The final couplet was,

> So gentle winds breed happy springs,
> And duty thrives by breath of kings.

On that day James obtained from the Earl of Salisbury, in exchange for the manor of Hatfield, the mansion of Theobalds in Hertfordshire, where he had often had good times. Built by the earl's father, William Cecil, it had curious buildings, lovely walks, and pleasant conceits within and without. Nevertheless, it was said that the shrewd earl gained by the bargain with the canny, grasping James.

With Parliament, which was growing more Puritan, James was ever in conflict, much of the time about money. The king was spending more and more on the costly trappings of the state as well as for his public and private pleasures. A court case had at length given him the long-withheld right to levy customs duties as he pleased, since, as it said, all affairs of commerce belonged to the king's power. While he delayed the levies, his debts grew. It was no wonder that he could pay his Bible translators only through the assignment of livings and minor incomes largely endowed.

The early years of James's reign, like the time of Elizabeth, saw many stirring ventures which would in due season help England to prosper. In 1607 a dozen rough, eager sea dogs, their captain among them, received the

Lord's Supper at St. Ethelburgh's, Bishopsgate, London. The tiny shop of a glover was cooped up in its porch. Nearby were taverns, the Angel, the Four Swans, the Queen's Head, and narrow, crooked alleys, such as those named Wormwood and Peahen. The rector was the Bible translator and Arabic scholar, Dr. William Bedwell, who was then hard at work also on his great Arabic lexicon. The captain with his seamen, about to set out on their voyage in the *Hopewell* to sail as they thought across the North Pole, was Henry Hudson.

In and around London on December 8, 1607, a hard frost set in and lasted for seven days, to impede movement. After a partial thaw, the frost got worse on the twenty-second. The Thames was so thickly covered with ice that it became the place for public fun. Coaches drove over the river as if it were dry land. Many set up booths and standings of sundry goods to sell upon the ice. On February 1 the ice at last began to break, the pressure breaking up many quaint wooden bridges, while floodwaters destroyed much wild fowl, fish, and herbage in gardens, such as artichokes and rosemary. Only in April did the freezing cease. No doubt in London, then as now ill-equipped for winter temperatures near zero, the translators at Westminster could hardly hold their books, papers, and pens, unless they hovered close to fireplaces.

The next year there were two more masques by Ben Jonson, the queen's masque on January 14, 1608, and in February the masque at Lord Hadington's marriage. There is no complaint of flimsy clothes at these. But when Queen Anne's brother, the king of Denmark, came to England for a state visit, he found ladies of the court too drunk to dance. They needed but gave no heed to Biblical sermons about wine as a mocker and strong drink as raging.

Teeming with commerce and population growth, London was undergoing a sort of building racket. "The itch of building continuing in defiance of the laws in being and the late proclamation, his majesty, looking upon the great increase of building in and about London as a rickety distemper in the head of the kingdom, which occasions a flux of humors and diseases to approach the court, and might in time bring the plague to Whitehall, did with the advice of his council again strictly prohibit the erecting buildings upon new foundations within two miles of the city, upon penalty of having them destroyed." Even the Westminster translators lived in fear of the plague, which many now supposed came partly from overcrowding and bad buildings. About how to dispose of sewage and other refuse people knew next to nothing.

In 1608 there was some difficulty about making Dr. John Harding, the Oxford translation chairman, president of Magdalen College. Thus Dr. Arthur Lake wrote, February 24, 1608, to his elder brother, Sir Thomas Lake, the king's secretary, "I have been to the Bishop of Winchester who will do his best to forward Dr. Harding, but there is a great conspiracy to exclude him." The two Lakes wrote to the vice-president and fellows of Magdalen College in Dr. Harding's behalf. At length Dr. Harding got the place, but lasted only a little over a year. Then Dr. Richard Kilby, another translator, replaced him.

In December, 1608, William Eyre, Emmanuel College, Cambridge, who sounds as if he were a translator, wrote a letter to James Ussher in Dublin, Ireland.[1] Eyre mentioned the pestilence in Cambridge, which must have alarmed the translators there, and the illness of Scaliger, the famous scholar and traveler, "with a dropsy and not like to escape death." Eyre asked that Ussher, because the new translation of the Bible was being hastened, return to him the copy of the part which he had lent to Ussher for a Dr. Daniel's use. The letter shows that there was an order from the king through the Archbishop of Canterbury, Bancroft, that the translation of the Bible be

[1] Ussher was later to prepare a chronology of Biblical events found in the reference columns of many editions of the King James Bible.

"finished and printed." That end was still a long way off.

During this same year there escaped from England to Amsterdam some of those who were to become the Plymouth Pilgrims, among them Elder William Brewster, perhaps William Bradford, and pastor John Robinson, who never reached America. Brewster and Robinson had been in college with some of the translators. Robinson must have known well John Overall and Laurence Chaderton.

The learned men kept on rising in their church world. On April 18, 1608, Arthur Lake, younger brother of the king's secretary, became Dean of Worcester. A year later, May 27, 1609, George Abbot, the prosy, dogged translator, became Bishop of Lichfield and Coventry. On December 14 of that year died the stringent but sociable translator, Thomas Ravis, Bishop of London, who had been. Dean of Christ Church. Before George Abbot could get used to Lichfield and Coventry, he became on February 12, 1610, Bishop of London, third in line from Richard Bancroft, who for six years had been Archbishop of Canterbury. All because Abbot's mother caught and ate a young pike while she waited for his birth, his advance to glory was steady and sure.

Meanwhile the king had many royal matters on his mind. He had to proclaim against "hunters, stealers, and killers of deer within any of the King's Majesty's forests, closes, or parks" at Hampton Court. Having built a new banquet house at Whitehall, he had celebrated with Jonson's *Masque of Queens.* Twelve women in the habits of hags and witches spoke such lines as,

> The owl is abroad, the bat and the toad
> And so is the cat-a-mountain,
> The ant and the mole sit both in a hole.

Old furies about witches had died down for a time; there had even been reprieves and pardons. In 1608 the Earl of Northampton as Warden of the Cinque Ports induced the Mayor of Rye to admit to bail a woman condemned to death for aiding a witch. Her hanging had been stayed; it was feared that she might succumb in the loathsome prison. That year also Simon Reade, a doctor and cunning man of Southwark, was pardoned after it was charged that he conjured and invoked unclean spirits. For the time being witches were more to amuse than to scare people.

The magical East India Company, first chartered by Queen Elizabeth in 1600, now received from King James a charter without limit of time. These were years for and of brilliance. Captain John Smith was off in Virginia. Captain Henry Hudson was about to sail up the lordly river that glories in his name. James took his queen, Anne, and the children to the Tower to see a treat of the lion's single valor against a great fierce bear which had killed another bear. So the romance and triviality of royal life went on while the translators slowly approached the end of their labors.

Now we revert to the translator John Overall, Dean of St. Paul's, who struggled with the profanations in Paul's Walk. When he was more than forty he had married a great beauty, Anne Orwell. They seem to have got on together for a time. Isaac Casaubon, who stayed with the Overalls in the dean's house, wrote letters mentioning Mrs. Overall in vague but kindly terms. At length of a sudden she ran away with a man named Sir John Selby. His name is all we know about him. Someone, or a number of men, chased the lovers along a road from London and brought the lady back to her husband. What the conflicts of the Overalls were or how the couple made out as they lived on in holy deadlock after the lady thus eloped and got caught we know not. Other wives of translators worried their husbands almost beyond bearing. Not all of the learned men profited by the advice of their fellow translator Francis Dillingham, who, though he never married, set forth how to keep a wife in proper subjection.

# CHAPTER 11

# The Good Word

In a time of intense conflict within and without the churches, the work on the Bible did not escape. One who in anger opposed it was the great Puritan Hebraist, Hugh Broughton. Broughton himself had urged a revised version and had hoped to be among those chosen for the work, but was left out because he was so acrid in his humors.

Broughton's first conflict had been with Edward Lively, the Cambridge translator, over Lively's time scheme for the Bible. Now he was bitter against Archbishop Bancroft and Bishop Bilson about the latter's thesis, the common belief of many churches today, that the soul of Jesus went for a short time to hell.

Bancroft, he said, "is a deadly enemy to both testaments and unallowable in this course to be a teacher or to rule in learning." In a pamphlet he went on with the attack on Bancroft, who had no love for him. "Tell his majesty,' he wrote among other things, "that I had rather be rent to pieces with wild horses than any such translation by my consent should be urged upon poor churches." The statement against Bancroft, the chief prelate in what was still Broughton's church, was addressed to the House of Lords. Now, in the reaction against the Puritans, Broughton was in danger, while Bancroft firmly managed the new Bible.

Among the papers of John Rainolds are some Broughton comments and advice set down with respect for his learning. Broughton made his own partial version of the Bible from which the King James men appear to have taken some wordings. Speaking of wild horses, Broughton said of the horse, in Job 39:19, "Canst thou clothe his neck with thunder?" The King James Bible asks, "Hast thou given the horse strength? Hast thou clothed his neck with thunder?" The English Revised Version has it, "Hast thou given the horse his might? Hast thou clothed his neck with the quivering mane?" No doubt this last conveys more of the Hebrew meaning. The King James men were working with, among other versions, the Bishops' Bible. That says oddly, "Hast thou given the horse his strength or learned him to neigh courageously?" This seems to be just a leaping guess at what appeared obscure. Yet all these wordings proclaim the power of God, and each has its rhythm and delight for us. Thunder is a figure for that which quivers; what a splendid phrase we lose if we object to "clothed his neck with thunder." We can thank rabid Hugh Broughton for his inspired word.

And as the work went on even Hugh Broughton was softening somewhat his thoughts about the new version. In 1609 he wrote, "None should bear sway in translating but the able." But he added, "The king's care to have the law and gospel learnedly translated hath stirred much study and expectation of good, and all true hearted subjects will be ready for forebearance."

It was, as we all know, a time of lambent English writing in other fields. Whitehall may have had Shakespeare's *Othello* on November 1, 1604. *King Lear* seems to date from 1605. Even Michael Drayton was writing his *Agincourt*—"Fair stood the wind for France"—and his ringing sonnet, "Since there's no help, come let us kiss and part." Samuel Daniel, along with his masques and other poems, wrote the lovely, expert sonnet, "Look, Delia, how we stem the half-blown rose." Raleigh, in the Tower, and Bacon were, as writers, in their prime. The blooming of even the minor Elizabethans appeared at its best while the translators labored, and may have given their hearts and minds some of its lushness. Yet the Bible and those flaming Elizabethans existed in realms apart.

Shakespeare seldom quoted or mentioned the Scriptures. There are, of course, words, phrases, and images common to both his plays and the Bible. In the earlier plays the promise of Deuteronomy 32:2, "My doctrine shall drop as the rain," has a parallel in Portia's description of mercy that "droppeth as the gentle rain from heaven." The rhetorical question, "What is man, that thou art mindful of him?" found in Psalm 8:4, and quoted in Hebrews 2:6, was echoed again in Hamlet's "What a piece of work is a man!" But these are similes and ideas inevitably occurring in works of such magnitude as the combined Old and New Testaments and the collected plays of Shakespeare.

If we compare the work done at the same time we find that while Bois, Downes, and the rest were shaping up the new Bible, Shakespeare was writing, had just written, or was about to write *The Winter's Tale, Cymbeline,* and *The Tempest.* There are no completed thoughts in these three plays that appear in the Bible too. Almost never in them does Shakespeare so much as arrange two words in any exact likeness to a Bible phrase. In *The Winter's Tale* there is a Biblical allusion in the line "my name be yoked with his that did betray the Best." In the same play one clause reads "lift up your countenance," inviting comparison with the Bible's "lift up his countenance." This is probably just a chance likeness. *The Winter's Tale* also contains a topical reference to a Puritan who sings psalms to hornpipes, but this shows mainly that Shakespeare did not take the Puritans seriously.

Indeed much writing of the age seemed opposed to the

Bible. Though George Chapman, for instance, often quoted the Scriptures, he also wrote in *Bussy D'Ambois,* 1607,

> Nature lays
> A deal of stuff together, use by use,
> Or by the mere necessity of matter,
> Ends such a work, fills it, or leaves it empty
> Of strength or virtue, error or clear truth,
> Not knowing what she does.

The Bible and the preachers had to do their utmost against such blasphemous talk, implying that nature, or matter, could evolve itself without divine purpose. Because of such speculations the translators had distrust for the writing of plays, lyrics, and profane pieces of most kinds, even though the king enjoyed them.

The age had countless contests between the lovely and the ugly, and the king's poor grandeur could further the worst and the best. Ben Jonson, who made so many masques for the king, could be vulgar in the extreme. He could also write, "Drink to me only with thine eyes." Thomas Campion, who wrote rather tawdry masques, wrote also "The man of life upright." Did Shakespeare have clean hands and a pure heart? His plays, especially in the bloodier and bawdier passages, cast doubt on that. Inner conflicts, or those in contemporary society, may be good for artists in words.

Yet the learned men, though together they made a masterpiece, were not primarily artists or men of letters, and the question remains how fifty to sixty men of as many minds achieved, in one great joint undertaking, the verbal felicities of the King James version. The king and his bishops who assigned the task apparently acted on the assumption that the work would be handled like any other churchly task, proceeding under authority from the lowest to the highest, at each stage to be approved by the next-ranking superior until it should reach the Crown.

Such a plan allowed little leeway for individual artistry in expression or even for inspiration.

When they went to work, the translators themselves outlined a more democratic procedure by which, after each had translated assigned passages, the proposed new version should be read aloud and listened to by the whole group, each hearer holding a different version of the passage for comparison. How well this plan of work was adhered to, after the start, it is difficult to say.

Yet we can discover a good deal about the way the learned men actually worked, and how carefully—they would have said *painfully*—they tried each word before setting it down. This knowledge we owe to notes made by John Bois of Cambridge.

Beginning probably some time in 1609, and continuing daily for three-fourths of a year, John Bois, Andrew Downes, and four others went daily to Stationers' Hall in London to revise the first draft of the Bible as it came from the groups in the universities and at Westminster.

Stationers' Hall was a plain structure of brick, with square casement windows and ovals above them. An iron railing enclosed the court before the building. A flight of stone steps in a circle led up to the grand entrance. Inside were good halls and rooms large and small. The place had a feeling of placid worth. There for hundreds of years nearly all who would bring out books had to "enter" them, and thus obtain certain rights—the beginning of today's copyright laws—to prevent pirating. Oddly, in the published lists of Stationers' Hall there is found no entry for the 1611 Bible, to which Robert Barker, the King's Printer, alone had any title.

Among the six men who went over the first drafts of the Bible manuscript at Stationers' Hall, besides Bois and Downes, were probably Arthur Lake and John Harmer. Arthur Lake, brother to the king's secretary, was born at St. Michael's, Southampton, in September, 1559, a son of Almeric Lake. He went to Winchester College, and was a fellow at New College, Oxford, where he became a doctor of divinity, May 16, 1605. In July, 1607, he was an archdeacon in Surrey, and in 1608 Dean of Worcester. An early written list, partly of queries, at Lambeth Palace mentions him among the translators. The Bois notes on their work refer here and there to AL, which of translators' initials could be only Arthur Lake. Conceivably the two letters stood, instead, for *alius* or *alii,* "one other" or "the others." However, in the notes for Philippians 4:1 we find *alii* spelled out, all in small letters. So Arthur Lake may have been one of the six men at Stationers' Hall.

John Harmer, whom Bois names, was born in Newbury, Berkshire, about 1555. The Earl of Leicester was his patron, and in 1569 got him into St. Mary's College, Winchester. In 1572 he transferred to New College, Oxford, where he had a scholarship, being of lowly parents. There he became a master of arts ten years later. Then, aided by Leicester, he went abroad and held disputations with great doctors of the Romish party. In 1585 Leicester had him made regius professor of Greek at Oxford. From 1588 to 1596 he was headmaster at Winchester. The next year he settled down for life as warden of St. Mary's. Meanwhile he was also rector at Droxford, Hampshire. Well read in patristic and scholastic theology, he was a most noted Latinist and Grecian. He rendered into English Calvin's sermon on the Ten Commandments. Clearly he was qualified to sit among the learned Bible men.

John Bois, or Boys, had been a student under Andrew Downes. On the new Bible both worked first in Cambridge on the Apocrypha, as we have seen, with John Duport, William Branthwaite, Jeremy Radcliffe, and the two Wards. When all the translators had prepared their versions, alone and in groups, Bois and Downes with the four others began their nine months' work on the whole in the daily meetings at Stationers' Hall.

An early account of the work at this stage is found in a life of Bois written by his friend and admirer, Anthony Walker.[1] "When it pleased God," Walker wrote, "to move King James to that excellent work, the translating of the Bible, when the translators were to be chosen for Cambridge, he (Bois) was sent for thither by those therein employed, and chosen one. Some university men thereat repining (it may be not more able, yet more ambitious to have a share in the service) and disdaining that it should be thought that they needed any help from the country, forgetting that Tully was the same at Tusculum that he was at Rome." Thus even at Cambridge some were jealous of Bois, who had his living outside the university.

"Sure I am," Walker went on, "that part of the Apocrypha was allotted to him (for he hath showed me the very copy that he translated by) but I know not what part thereof. All the time he was about his own part his diet was given to him at St. John's [College] where he abode all the week till Saturday night and then went home to discharge his cure, returning thence on Monday morning."

A little instance of further conflict follows. "When he had finished his own, at the earnest request of him to whom it was assigned, he undertook a second part, and then was in commons at another college. But I will forbear to name both the person and the house. Four years[2] he spent in this service, at the end whereof (the whole work being finished and three copies of the whole Bible being sent to London, one from Cambridge, a second from Oxford, and a third from Westminster) a new choice was to be made of six in all, two of each company, to review the whole work, and extract one out of all three, to be committed to the press. For the dispatch of this business,

[1] Included in Francis Peck's *Desiderata Curiosa*. London, 1779.
[2] The "four years" seem to have been from late 1604 or early 1605 to late 1608 or early 1609, and the three-fourths of a year to have been in 1609, or perhaps a little into 1610.

Master Downes and he, out of the Cambridge company, were sent for up to London, where meeting their four fellow laborers, they went daily to Stationers Hall, and in three quarters of a year fulfilled their task. . . . Whilst they were conversant in this last business, he (Bois) and he only took notes of their proceedings, which he diligently kept to his dying day."

Walker added that the six received daily "thirteen shillings each of them by the week from the company of stationers, though before they had nothing." The tall, rugged Downes was stubbornly bent on getting more, and sometimes avowed that he would go to Stationers' Hall only if he was fetched or threatened with a pursuivant bearing a warrant for arrest. He doubtless believed that his travel on account of the Bible should be at public expense. We may conclude that Church and state told Downes and any others with mercenary thoughts to get on with what they had to do.

However, there are papers to show that Downes had long been aggrieved and "humbly resolved" to get his due, with some small success. In 1608 Downes had sent to the king a humble plea about the maintenance of the Lady Margaret's divinity lecture which he gave at Cambridge. He said that he had been the king's professor of Greek now for almost two and twenty years, "employed beside in the translation and put to the greatest and hardest part of all," referring to the revision he was about to undertake, and had "not yet received any consideration for it, as others gave my inferiors far more in time and pains." He had looked and hoped all this while to be remembered with the others, but seeing young men preferred before him, "and myself still left behind," he was "driven at the last" to speak for himself. "I have been the king's professor so long," continually conversant with all ancient authors, and with Latin and Greek—he did not mention the Hebrew learned at five—"it will not seem I trust unreasonable for me the king's reader to have some allowance out of that ample portion assigned to the Lady Margaret's reader till I can be better provided for." He was thus direct in asking for a good part of the sum given for the Lady Margaret's reader, 160 pounds. At last, on May 17, 1609, a royal grant "in regard of his pains" bestowed on him fifty pounds as a "free gift and reward."

This seems to have been the only cash that any translator received from the king. The wages paid at Stationers' Hall, nine pounds a week for the six men, for nine months, came to £360. It is certain only that this money did not come from the Crown. Did the Worshipful Company of Stationers advance the amount for a worthy project, out of the goodness of their hearts? (Not long before, they had subscribed £125 toward founding the colony of Virginia, and five years later would give £45 more.) It seems more likely that Robert Barker, already licensed to publish, advanced the money through the company, of which at about this time he was Master. The amount was only a little more than a tenth of what he would spend, all told, on the new Bible. And at any rate the Stationers provided working space.

If we try to determine the identity of the half dozen, besides Bois and Downes, John Harmer and possibly Arthur Lake, the notes mention Hutchinson, presumably of the original group working on the New Testament at Westminster. But a reference does not prove that the translator named was working at Stationers' Hall; the men there could have been discussing work done earlier. Bois's biographer says only that at Stationers' Hall they started afresh, not with those who had previously been overseers or supervisors of the groups.

Harmer had translated into English certain sermons by the French scholar Beza, who followed Calvin at Geneva and published a New Testament in Latin. Beza's influence on the work of the translators has been noted by scholars, and besides Harmer's direct contributions to the Bois jottings, the several references to Beza may have been made at his instigation. AL also is quoted, but the most frequent contributor of recommended readings is Downes. Downes and Bois were old working partners, having been master and student in the early days of Greek scholarship at Oxford, and together assisting Sir Henry Savile in his mammoth translation of St. Chrysostom.

Thus as the six men worked their daily stint, presumably around a table piled with papers and books of reference, the readings recommended by the scholars at Oxford and Cambridge and Westminster, and the Bibles already translated into English and Latin as well as the original Hebrew and the variant texts in Greek, we can see Bois keeping his faithful notes—scribbling away at the pages still preserved for us in the Oxford copy. We can hear Downes—"our most subtle thinker in words," Bois called him—compare one Greek reading with another, discuss the position of modifiers, or decide which preposition should be supplied to fit the needs of English grammar. Did he, as was his habit when lecturing at his own college, lounge with his long legs on the table? Or did he, in deference to the company and their solemn task, sit more decorously; and then, baffled by a puzzling construction in St. Paul, stand and walk about, perhaps stare at his own reflection in a window made a mirror by the black London fog, and think how we "see in a glass darkly"?

Bois's notes run from Romans through the Apocalypse, and for the debatable passages present a number of alternate readings. At Stationers' Hall the work was still in the stage of searching for the right word or combination of words to express an idea, and even of deciding which idea to adopt, among the possibilities suggested by the different translations or inherent in the different grammatical structure of the ancient texts. So Bois put down

[*115*]

word meanings as a dictionary would, or alternates as a thesaurus would; later still would come a choice among possible constructions for sound and rhythm and euphony of the whole. The Bois notes show how careful the translators were, first of all, to determine exact meanings or establish a permissible range of meaning.

Final constructions thus appear, almost always, to simplify the Bois suggestions. Thus in Romans 3:9 the notes suggest: "What then? Are we safe and out of danger? Are we preferred? Are we God's darlings?" The King James question is "What then? Are we better than they?"

In I Corinthians 9:18 Bois offered: "that I strain not to the utmost my power in the gospel, or that I rack not, or stretch not, etc." The King James reading is, "that I abuse not my power in the gospel.'

Andrew Downes in I Corinthians 10:20 proposed: "and I would not have you partakers with the devil." The 1611 Bible said, "and I would not that ye should have fellowship with devils." Here as elsewhere Downes' comments are in Latin, and long, as he filtered the sense from the Greek through the Latin, the language of scholars. The plural "devils," by the way, seems better than "devil" in the passage, for it appears to mean little demons rather than the great fiend or Satan. The Revised Standard Version uses "demons."

Chapter 15, verse 33 of I Corinthians we all know well. Downes wanted "good manners," "good natures," or "good dispositions." The learned men at last settled on the first of these: "Be not deceived: evil communications corrupt good manners."

For II Corinthians 2:10 Bois proposed "in the person, in the sight or in the name of Christ." The 1611 Bible uses a Bois word in its reading, "in the person of Christ." For 5:3, the Bois suggestion was "if so be that we shall be found clothed, and not naked." The king's Bible changes the order: "if so be that being clothed we shall not be found naked." For 5:19 Bois put down "that God in Christ reconciled the world." The 1611 Bible reads "that God was in Christ, reconciling the world unto himself." Here the changes are small and mainly of grammar and rhythm, but again we see the fusing of the 1611 Bible going on as we read.

In the final editing the last learned men, Smith and Bilson, used the Bois words "perfecting holiness" in II Corinthians 7:1. In the next verse they refused the Bois phrasing, "we have made a gain of no man," in favor of "we have wronged no man." For 8:4 they took the whole Downes reading, "that we would receive the gift, and take upon us the fellowship of the ministering to the saints."

A near miss by Bois is in II Corinthians 9:5 where he recommended, "as a bounty and not as a thing extorted." The 1611 Bible reads "as a matter of bounty, and not as of covetousness." The Revised Standard Version chose "not as an exaction but as a willing gift," which is better, and nearer Bois, than the 1611 wording.

Trying phrases for Galatians 4:15, Bois wrote: "What is become then of the happiness that was ascribed unto you, of your magnifying of yourselves, of thinking yourselves happy for my sake, your happiness that is talked of or spoken of?" Many a writer thus tries many phrasings. The reading finally adopted was "Where is then the blessedness ye spake of?"

In Philippians Bois tendered for 1:19, "the bounty of the Spirit." The final version reads "the supply of the Spirit." For 1:21 he set down "life unto me is Christ, and death an advantage." The king's Bible chose one-syllable words: "To me to live is Christ, and to die is gain." For Philippians 2:20 Bois and AL suggested, "no man like minded . . . who will truly be careful of your matters, or careful from the heart." Andrew Downes, struggling hard with Paul's Greek, made literal notes: "so dear unto me, whom I love of my own soul." The 1611 Bible says with greater ease, "I have no man like-minded who will naturally care for your state."

For the well-known Philippians 3:14, Bois offered: "I follow directly to the price (prize) of the high calling . . ." and AL proposed, "I follow toward the mark for the price (prize). . . ." We all know that the King James verse reads, "I press toward the mark for the prize of the high calling of God in Christ Jesus."

Bois suggested for Philippians 3:20, "your city in heaven" or "heaven for our city." This illustrates the difficulty with connectives, lacking in the Greek text and sometimes requiring a decision as to the meaning of a phrase, a clause, or a sentence. Here the final King James version is the phrase much used, "our conversation is in heaven." To Elizabethans "conversation" meant much more than talk; it was the action of living or having one's being in and among. The Revised Standard Version has it "our commonwealth is in heaven," which accedes somewhat to the Bois concept of "city."

In I Thessalonians 5:23, Downes proposed "that your spirit may be kept perfect." The king's Bible has, "your whole spirit . . . be preserved blameless." The Revised Standard Version says, ". . . be kept sound and blameless."

"May be schooled not to blaspheme" was what Bois offered for I Timothy 1:20. The king's Bible says, "that they learn not to blaspheme"; this stresses learning where Bois stressed teaching. Another rare passage in which the meaning was changed in revision is II Timothy 2:5, for which Downes recommended, "and though a man labor for the best gain, try masteries . . . unless he strive and labor lustily." The King James Bible says, "And if a man also strive for masteries, yet is he not crowned, except he strive lawfully." The Revised Standard has, "An athlete is not crowned unless he competes according to the rules."

The word "strive" or "contend" is, in the Greek, the word from which we get "athlete," one who strives in the public lists. The passage is a demand that one follow the rules of the game, but Downes missed the point that the verse refers to a contest of athletes.

We may assume that the scriptural passages for which Bois made no notes passed on to Smith and Bilson from the first draft without much change. Yet we must not suppose that the Bois notes preserved to us are more than hints of all that he, Downes, and the other four worked over; the forty pages of these notes are but a teasing fragment. At the end, someone has written: "These notes were taken by John Bois, one of the translators of the king's Bible," and added that they were "transcribed out of a copy by some unskilled hand, very confused and faulty, especially in the Greek." But the notes are not faulty in Greek, only terse and stenographic. Perhaps the annotator did not like Bois's ligatured Greek writing, which shortly went out of style.

But are there any other such notes about the making of a true world masterpiece? Why should these have survived when we have nothing comparable from Shakespeare?

Commentators have pored over the only other material evidence, available in another form—that copy of the Bishops' Bible which is cherished in the Bodleian Library, with marginal notes for suggested changes inked in. Yet the changes are not always those of the King James version, and may have been those of an amateur working independently with the zeal so widely felt. If they were made by one of the Oxford translators it would be interesting to see whether the phrases which differ from the final version are among those discussed by Bois.

There are various interpretations of the nature of the work done at Stationers' Hall and its importance to the whole undertaking, especially with reference to the final editing done by Miles Smith and Bishop Bilson. Read carefully, the Bois notes show at least two things: first, that at this stage the work was still subject to changes, and second, that to the very end the learned men tried and tried again, so that we can share the very creakings of their thoughts.[3] Thus the notes which Bois "diligently kept to his dying day" seem to warrant attention, although apparently they have never been published.

Nor did the work of the Stationers' Hall men end with the printing of the 1611 Bible. Minor revisions were made after the first edition, having to do chiefly with uniform usage of a different type face to distinguish the connective words added to make better sense in English. John Bois himself was concerned with such small revisions as late as the Cambridge Revised Edition of 1638.

All these efforts with word meanings are of course laborious and, in the case of Scripture, highly important. Bois's biographer said, "Surely it will be easily granted that a man of a pregnant fancy and ready invention may sooner, and with more ease, write a leaf of his own than he can examine a line, it may be a word, of a decayed, crabbed author, or a dark manuscript which perchance cannot be done without perusing twenty more." Bois it was whose father taught him Hebrew at a tender age; his mother, a bluestocking of her period, had read the Bible through twelve times, presumably in the Geneva version. This sort of patience and piety the men at Stationers' Hall had and needed.

Yet their notes are evidence only of the essential spadework, the digging away at roots to lay a firm foundation. We still have no sure answer for that final choice and

[3] Dr. Frederick C. Grant of Union Theological Seminary, New York, upon seeing the notes, observed a parallel with his own experience in work on the Revised Standard Version: "The King James translators faced many problems that we did—or rather, we faced those which they faced, long ago. One can almost hear the committee at work."

Cap.7.15. He shall pitch his tent over them. he shall protect them. he shall dwell with them, he shall rest upon them, shall rule over them σκηνώσει αυτοις. umbraculo prote-get eos vide 2 Cor 12.9. rest upon me. i.e. Aretha interprete. ενοικησει κη ιπερεγισαιτιοτει αυτοις. vide infra c.12.12. c.21.3. et c.13.6.

Cap.8.13. by reason of the rest etc. vide c.9.2. εν τω χωντε.

Cap.10.9. and it shall offend thy belly.

Cap.11.10. shall feast, shall make merry, A.D. δωρα. i.e. αποσολης

Ibid v.17 and hast entred thy kingdome.

Ibid v.18 destroy them that destroy, or corrupt    Anta-naclasis. vide 1. Cor 3.17

Cap.12.4. ευρε. pro ευρε. ινα οταν τεκη, that as soon as she was delivered.

Ibid v.9. εβληθη, ie εξεβληθη

Ibid v.10. εγινετο] ie. forte. παρεγινετο.

Ibid v.11 for the bloud, because of the bloud.

Cap.13.3. εσφαγμενω etc. sauciatum, πληγεισαν, improprie.

Ibid v.5. to continue. i.e. διατριψαι or, to make warre, ποιησαι πολεμον Al. in Manuscripto, πολεμησαι D Harmer.

Ibid v.8. A.D. et Hutch. contendebant το απο κατα-βολης κοσμου conjungendum esse potius cum γεγραπται quam cum εσφαγμενου: quorum sententiae aperto favet Arethas, si modo recte eum intelligo, vide c.17.8. Ceterum cum omnes quod sciam interpretes, et bona pars Expositorum tam veterum quam recent. hunc locum intelligunt de aeternitate sacrificii Christi, non arbitror tutum in re tam trita et pervulgata aliquid καινοτομειν.    [v. 21.27.

Ibid v.10. into Captivity etc. vide Mat.26.52.

Ibid v.12. ενωπιον αυτου ] like unto him, A.D. Arethas, ενωπιον δε οιονει, ακολουθως αυτω, καθ ουδεν παραλλαττον της παρουσιας το πρωτη ελθανα

Ibid.

A page of the Bois notes, reproduced by permission of the President and Fellows of Corpus Christi College, Oxford.

arrangement of words that makes the Bible translated for the king tower above the rest.

In evaluating the work of the editors, some have supposed that the men at Stationers' Hall did most of the real work and that Miles Smith and Bishop Bilson, although they went over the work once more before it was sent to the printer, merely approved a final version submitted to them, and wrote the chapter headings.

Another possibility, however, is that the men at Stationers' Hall were concerned chiefly with disputed meanings, and that they served as expert arbitrators between variants—not only those proposed by the earlier readings made by the translators in groups, but variants in the original texts. Then Smith and Bilson presumably reworked the raw material of acceptable meanings into the smooth vibrant prose of the printed version.

No way of settling these questions of literary credit now suggests itself. The Bois notes, if taken to represent the work at Stationers' Hall—as seems entirely reasonable —strongly support the second assumption, because the readings offered differ from the final King James version. Also there are usually several readings, indicating that Bois put down possible alternates rather than final selections. When none of the Bois words is identical with the final readings, there is today no way of telling whether additional work at Stationers' Hall inserted the accepted phrase in the manuscript, whether Smith and Bilson found it, or whether the final reading was one chosen by the group originally assigned to translate the passage.

The time schedule is no help because, although the Stationers' Hall work went on for nine months and so lasted longer than Smith and Bilson worked afterwards, we cannot know whether the work overlapped; Smith and Bilson may well have started while the men at Stationers' Hall continued. Thus the range of possibility is from a board of final editors at Stationers' Hall, with Smith and

Bilson giving nominal approval, to the hypothesis that the men at Stationers' Hall were mainly concerned with problems of verbal meaning, with a final editing to supply "polish"—in this case, the poetic rhythm so important in the King James Bible.

All we know is that somewhere within the range of talents at work on the 1611 Bible were those necessary for a good and complete translation, one that would represent the original writing in a new language in quality as well as in sense. It is often said that a good translation should be done by at least two people, one a linguist to provide literal meanings, one a skilled writer to look out for cadence and style. Thus today it might be suggested that the Isaiah of the Dead Sea Scrolls would be best translated into English by a learned philologist plus an English stylist of the rank of Christopher Fry. If we apply this reasoning to the King James Bible it seems clear that Bois and Downes, and perhaps the other four at Stationers' Hall, were the linguists supplying various supportable renderings of the difficult passages. There may have been artists in words, too, among them; certainly there were talented men among the translators who had worked at Oxford and Cambridge and Westminster. But what if Miles Smith, with or without real help from Bishop Bilson, had still to make literature of the result?

# CHAPTER 12

# The Final Touches

A story goes that someone put all those commas and colons into the King James Bible, and made the verse and chapter divisions, while riding horseback. If there is any truth in it, the guilty man may have been Dr. Miles Smith, who used to keep at work even on journeys, jogging along on a jennet. Many a stop breaks up a long, loping verse at random.

One comma in Isaiah 9:6 has enjoyed especial fame: "For unto us a child is born, unto us a son is given; and the government shall be upon his shoulder: and his name shall be called Wonderful, Counselor, The mighty God, The everlasting Father, The Prince of Peace." As we read that, we can hear the music of Handel's *Messiah*. It is splendid verse in groups of balanced words. But the comma does not belong between "Wonderful" and "Counselor":

> And his name shall be called
> Wonderful Counselor,
> The Mighty God,
> The Everlasting Father,
> The Prince of Peace.

Alas, if we leave out the comma, we lose that wondrous pause in *The Messiah* between the two words!

Music meant less in the England of James than in the

England of Elizabeth, and Handel had yet to come. But music was in the air around, and the rhythms of the King James version are such that, whether or not the verses are set to music, most people seem to recognize that they are poetry. Somewhere, somehow, in the process of translation the prosaic, labored definitions of the original translators and later of Downes and Bois were arranged in rhythms that were to last.

As an example of how this was done, consider that one verse in the brilliant I Corinthians 13 received from Bois five painstaking readings. For verse 11 he proposed "I understood, I cared as a child, I had a child's mind, I imagined as a child, I was affected as a child." The King James Bible says, in words that have become fixed for us with a gravely swinging rhythm, "I spake as a child, I understood as a child, I thought as a child." Would the "imagined as a child" offered by Downes suffice instead of "understood as a child"? The rhythm is much the same.

Many have discussed the use, in I Corinthians 13, of the word "charity" for the Greek *agape*. We have no light on how the learned men came to prefer this word to the word "love" which appears in some older versions. The Bishops' Bible, before that of Geneva, used "charity." Taste has shifted back and forth between the words in that fine chapter of Paul, and will doubtless shift again as the overtones of definition change. But if we can, as we read I Corinthians, divest the word "charity" of rather smug later meanings, we can sense a fitness in its rhythm.

Rhythm in the days of King James was important not merely as a source of pleasure to the ear, but as an aid to the mind. Generations to come would learn to read by puzzling out verses in the Bible that for many families would be a whole library. But at the time of translation, a Bible "appointed to be read in churches" was made to be listened to and remembered. Its rhythms were important as a prompting for memory. For that reason, in the words of their own Bible, it is evident that the learned men learned to use their ears as they worked—"the ear trieth words as the mouth tasteth meat."

There were other tests which the Bible editors used. They remembered that their purpose was to make an English translation, and though many of them could think in the ancient tongues, their King James Bible is indeed English. A striking instance is the word "righteous," which comes from the older English Bibles, and means right-wise. The Lord our righteousness is the Lord our right-wiseness, a profound meaning which is but faintly in the Hebrew and the Greek. Thus in many cases the English added content as well as form. But the English words as such were preferred. This led naturally to approval of a large proportion of the Tyndale translation in preference to the Bishops' Bible recommended in the royal directive. The simple, straightforward words of Tyndale appealed to the 1611 editors as they do to us today, so that his New Testament and Pentateuch have come down almost intact, except for minor changes. In the choice of phrasings from Stationers' Hall a similar standard prevailed.

Thus, chapter 2:15, of II Timothy in the 1611 Bible is, "Study to show thyself approved unto God, a workman that needeth not to be ashamed, rightly dividing the word of truth." Bois offered three choices: "a faithful laborer, a constant laborer, a laborer not ashamed of his work." The last editors preferred the English word "workman" to the Latin "laborer."

The date of the English words used also was considered. For Titus 2:10 Bois gave a vivid term, "no filchers," which was changed to "not purloining." "To filch" dates from 1561 and was early Elizabethan slang, whereas "to pur-loin" dates from 1440 and must have seemed more proper for Holy Scriptures. The King James Bible includes few words that were novel in 1611.

For Titus 3:8, Bois, who seems sometimes to have been

a bit earthy, said "be careful to exercise themselves in honest trades." The 1611 Bible says, "be careful to maintain good works." Andrew Downes suggested, for verse 14, "to profess, to practice honest trades." The published verse reads, "learn to maintain good works for necessary uses." These readings suggest that the final editors disliked the word "trades." Yet they could be businesslike. When for verse 17 of Philemon, Bois tendered "If thou thinkest all things common between us, if mine be thine and thine mine,' Smith and Bilson approved the prosy "If thou count me therefore a partner."

Beyond thought and skill in the choice of words, and beyond even the rhythmic patterns that make poetry, the learned men had to think of meaning. At about this time Francis Bacon, Lancelot Andrewes' friend, was warning: "Whereas the meaning ought to govern the term, the term in effect governeth the meaning." An important duty of the translators was to see that this did not happen. But this required agreement on meaning—if not "mine thine and thine mine, with all things common between us," then at least a working partnership. For the six linguists at Stationers' Hall this must have been easier than for the many men of varying views in the colleges and at Westminster. But the doctrinal implications of the words they dealt with must have occasioned many discussions during the nine months.

Perhaps it was no accident that the two final editors differed in their views, for thus they could best represent the whole group of translators and, indeed, the readers for whom all worked. Of the two, Miles Smith was not unfriendly to the Puritan point of view and in after years acted a good deal in accord with it. Bishop Bilson was a dullish, dogged churchman; yet the two balanced each other and represented their times.

About the basic issues they could agree. As a whole their great work was of course Protestant, against the

Church of Rome, which was even then, at Douay in France, publishing its own revised Old Testament in English. Its translators were mostly expatriate Catholics from Oxford, one of them John Rainolds' brother William. On September 7, 1608, the leading English Catholic, Birkhead, wrote a letter to Dr. Thomas Worthington, president of Douay College. Birkhead, who for safety signed with an alias, George Lambton, said "I am glad the Bible is so forward." The complete Douay Bible came out in 1610, a year ahead of the King James version.

The Douay Bible often has its sturdy charm. Yet it differs remarkably from the King James Bible. In Psalm 23 it reads, "Thou hast anointed my head with oil, and my chalice which inebriateth me, how goodly it is!" Psalm 91 begins, "He that dwelleth in the aid of the most High shall abide under the protection of the God of Jacob." Verse 13 says "Thou shalt walk upon the asp and the basilisk." Isaiah 61:1 starts, "Arise, be enlightened, O Jerusalem." At places it seems almost as if the Roman and the King James Bibles had determined to make their words differ as much as they could, to show that their standpoints were poles apart.

Fortunately for their text, the King James men were in somewhat better agreement, yet they differed to the end. Miles Smith, as final editor, protested that after he and Bilson had finished, Bishop Bancroft made fourteen more changes. "He is so potent there is no contradicting him," said Smith, and cited as an example of Bancroft's bias his insistence on using "the glorious word bishopric" even for Judas, in Acts 1:20: "His bishopric let another take."

The fact that Smith was the one to protest Bancroft's amendments suggests that he stood against both Bilson and Bancroft in such matters as the importance of bishoprics. Yet there is some reason to believe that if he stood alone, Smith was more than a match for his associates. He was admitted to be a modest man yet a hard worker, and these combined traits could have given him the opportunity to do a great deal to the work about which he had —except for possible interference from Bilson or Bancroft—the final say.

While others among the translators won praise for pulpit eloquence or strength in argument, there is evidence that Smith could write directly and to the point. Besides his sermons, which reveal too little of his real talents, we have the preface that he wrote for the Bible. Regrettably, those who publish the 1611 Bible now as a rule leave it out. It remains a good piece of writing, well worth reading for what it says as well as an example of what Miles Smith could do with words.

The whole task of translation could hardly be better described than in Smith's terse statement of purpose, "to deliver God's book unto God's people in a tongue which they understand." This talent for summarizing, for cutting through verbiage to say what was meant with force and the fewest possible words, was exactly what must have been needed at this stage of the work, and it was a talent Smith had. He also had the imagination to grasp a meaning not immediately obvious, and make it clear, as when he quoted St. Augustine's "A man would rather be with his dog than with a stranger," and explained the *stranger* as one "whose tongue is strange unto him." Finally, the very structure of his sentences as well as their content proves that Smith had energy and determination, what he described—in a phrase to find an echo in the American Constitution—as "zeal to promote the common good."

Again and again the final version shortens or changes the careful phrasing of Stationers' Hall to one of the memorable homely phrases of the King James version. Thus for Hebrews 4:15, where Andrew Downes suggested, "such an one as had experience of all things," the final reading became, "in all points tempted like as we are."

When for Hebrews 6:6 Bois offered, "caused him to be had in derision, or traduced him," the king's Bible says, "put him to an open shame."

For a famous verse, Hebrews 11:1, Bois put down, "Faith is a most sure warrant of things, is a being of things hoped for, a discovery, a demonstration of things that are not seen." This became, "Now faith is the substance of things hoped for, the evidence of things not seen."

Sometimes the considerations of rhythm, sound of letters, and homely English were combined in the changes. Thus for Hebrews 11:3, "Things which are seen were not made of things which do appear," replaced Bois's phrase "made of things that were not extant." Perhaps the word "extant" sounded fancy, and also the three t's are unattractive. Later in the same chapter, however, the final editing slipped into heavy alliteration in the phrase of verse 26, "he had respect unto the recompense of the reward." Bois had written only, "He looked at the reward to be rendered," and the Revised Standard Version prefers Bois, saying simply, "he looked to the reward."

The learned men who finished the work had great skill with the little words that connect the main words. They used them to give swing to their phrases. Many have remarked on their taste with short words, on how they made them pliant. About this they knew much more than those who had dealt with the English Bible before them. They tried their best to have their words fitly joined.

Now and then as they smoothed the Bois phrases they made a real change in meaning, as when the Bois phrase for Hebrews 12:2, "the leader and finisher of our faith," became "the author and finisher of our faith." But mainly the editing supplied more direct sentence structure and subtler groupings and rhythms. When Bois suggested for Hebrews 12:12, "lift up your slack hands and feeble or shaking knees," the finished Bible reads "lift up the hands which hang down, and the feeble knees." When in chapter 13:8 Bois put down, "yesterday and today the same and forever," we have from a hearing ear, "the same yesterday and today and forever," For Bois's phrase in verse 21, "disposing of you, or working with you as it pleaseth him," the final reading is "working in you that which is well-pleasing in his sight."

Now and then a phrase with original meaning based on a simile proved untranslatable, as when in James 1:5 Bois's literal rendering of the Greek, "twitting or hitting in the teeth"—with a sense of casting in the teeth—became "upbraideth not." Similarly in James 2:10, Bois's verb "trip," rendering a Greek verb meaning to fall down, became "offend in one point" of the law. But when for verse 8 of the first chapter Bois said "a wavering man," final editing supplied a more concrete image: "a double-minded man."

Occasionally different words were chosen to avoid repetition. For I Peter 3:14 Bois said, "fear not their fear, nor be troubled," and AL suggested "be not afraid of their fear." The final version reads, "be not afraid of their terror, neither be troubled." Such changes make appropriate the verse in II Peter 1:19 for which Bois wrote "and (hereby) we have the word," and AL said, "and hereby the speeches of the prophets are more confirmed unto us, are made of greater credit unto us, a more firm speech, etc." The edited reading is, "We have also a more sure word of prophecy."

For the complexities of Revelation, Bois really exerted himself. Thus for 7:15 he proposed, "He shall pitch his tent over them, he shall protect them, he shall dwell with them, he shall rest upon them, he shall rule over them," and in a note he added one more reading, "He shall stretch his pavilion over them." The approved reading adapted Bois's third and simplest reading, "He shall dwell among them." For chapter 19:9, AL translated "These true sayings are of God.' For the king's Bible, the master rhythmists changed this to "These are the true sayings of God."

The final editors had also to supply punctuation and decide questions of grammar, unless they were able to find helpers for the work which today would be called "copy editing." Some points of grammar in the King James Bible have bothered readers more than they did the men of 1611, who like the Elizabethans wrote with the freedom of a language still more or less fluid. What to Christians is perhaps the greatest question of all time reads ungrammatically, in Matthew 16:13, "Whom do men say that I, the Son of man, am?" English grammar has never been static; then as always it was growing and the use of pronouns was changing. "It is me" is today accepted by many experts in grammar, and here *me* is a usage comparable to the *whom*. With their feeling for sound, it is possible that the translators considered it far less objectionable than "Who do . . . ?"

Some other points of grammar in the King James Bible require us simply to forbear in adverse judgment. Elizabethan grammar has a charm of its own, even when a wrong pronoun gives a comic effect; in I Kings 13:27, the 1611 Bible says, "And he spake unto his sons, saying, Saddle me the ass. And they saddled *him*." The "him" is in italics to indicate that it is not in the original Hebrew, so there can be no argument when subsequent versions change "him" to "it."

Whether Smith and Bilson attended only to the final details of publishing scripts that were nearly complete except for disputed passages worked over at Stationers' Hall, or whether they are to be credited with a final editing that made the King James version into literature, cannot be decided from the data now at hand. From the first there were among the translators, as we have seen, men hailed in their own time as masters of language, sweet preachers, persuasive, and of a pretty wit. Rainolds,

Andrewes, Savile, Layfield, Bing—any of these, and several others, might well have contributed chapters so well turned as to require no rewriting. The difficulty is that, to a modern reader, the thought occurs that nothing in all their many volumes of sermons and other writing seems to march with the Bible cadence quite as does the prefatory address to the reader written by Miles Smith. On this similarity (which does not extend to his sermons) must rest any case for saying that Smith brought to the final editing its real inspiration.

The 1611 Bible had also to be prefaced by an address to the king. We do not know who addressed James as "Your majesty . . . the principal Mover and Author of the work." The task of this writing would have been considered an honor, and must have been one congenial to Bishop Bilson, perhaps with help from Bancroft. In his preface to the reader, which even contained a polite reference to Bishop Bancroft, Miles Smith said simply and fairly: "And what can the King command to be done, that will bring him more true honor than this?"

# The Bible Printed

There was no competition for the job of printing the new Bible. It went to Robert Barker, the royal printer, who also published it. His father, Christopher Barker, had received from Queen Elizabeth the sole right to print English Bibles, books of common prayer, statutes, and proclamations. On the death of Christopher Barker in 1599 the queen had given to his son, Robert Barker, the office of Queen's Printer for life with the same monopoly. The Barkers and their heirs held the private right to publish the King James Bible for a hundred years.[1]

Also from the Crown, Robert Barker had received in 1603 a lease on the manor of Upton, near Windsor, for twenty years at a rental of twenty pounds a year. Both father and son lived in London at Bacon House in Noble Street, Aldersgate. Their printing shop was nearby in St. Paul's churchyard at the sign of the Tiger's Head, a device on the arms of Sir Francis Walsingham, the friend of the Puritans. Thus we may assume that the Barkers shared in the Puritan trend.

For the new Bible Robert Barker laid out £3500, a large sum even for the royal printer. He appears to have obtained a new cast type, boldface for the text, with lighter Roman letters for the words which have no coun-

[1] It was Barker who in 1631 printed the so-called "Wicked Bible" with the error which omitted *not* from the seventh commandment.

terpart in the ancient-language texts but which the learned men had to insert for making sense in English. (In modern editions such words are printed in italic type.) The engraved title page shows Moses and Aaron standing in niches with the seated figures of Matthew, Mark, Luke, and John at the corners. This is signed C. Boel—Cornelius Boel, an Antwerp artist. Alas, this 1611 Bible omitted the full-page Garden of Eden, with all the fierce and harmless creatures lying around, that was in the Bishops' Bible. However, the whole is a handsome, well-printed folio. The linen and rag paper, after more than three hundred years, is tough and pleasant to look at and to touch. The first issue is today as easy to read as ever, though the type face, of course, is antiquated.

Of the actual printing we know nothing. Who were the humble printers, the craftsmen? Who read the proof? How long did the great process take? What was the selling price? There were two printings of the new Bible in 1611. How many copies were there of each issue? These are questions for which others may sometime find answers.

We do know that Miles Smith and Thomas Bilson, Bishop of Winchester, saw the volume through the press. Conceivably they read proofs. The handwritten copy from which the printers worked remained in Barker's possession, though there were complaints against his keeping it. In time it vanished.

There were, of course, mistakes made by the printers, averaging about one in ten pages. The first folio was known as the "He" Bible from a confusion of pronouns in Ruth 3:15, which made the verse end "and he went into the city." Corrected, the second folio became the "She" Bible.

What of the first copies off the press? Did Miles Smith and any or all of the other translators get a free copy of the new Bible? Did they or their churches have to buy copies?

We may even ask, did Smith have a copy at hand to use? Let us look at some of his sermons, published in 1632, after his death. It is not certain when the sermons were composed but it seems likely that most of them were delivered after 1612. Some of them he may have written while the 1611 Bible was in progress. We would expect that he, of all men, would quote from the work to which he gave his skill.

However, when he preached on Jeremiah 9:23, 24, the wording of his text differed at two points from that of the King James Bible. Smith said: "Let not the wise man glory in his wisdom, nor the strong man glory in his strength, neither the rich man glory in his riches; but let him that glorieth glory in this, that he understandeth and knoweth me." The 1611 Bible used *mighty* and *might* for *strong* and *strength,* and there are other, slighter changes.

When Smith quoted Zechariah 1:5, 6, he also used an older version: "Your fathers, where are they? And do the prophets live for ever? But did not my words and my statutes, which I commanded by my servants the prophets, take hold of your fathers?" Here the King James translators changed the order of the phrases.

For his sermon on Jeremiah 6:16 Smith used the exact words of the King James Bible: "Thus saith the Lord, Stand ye in the ways, and see, and ask for the old paths, where is the good way, and walk therein, and ye shall find rest for your souls." But he shortened and simplified Ecclesiastes 10:1, saying, "Dead flies corrupt the ointment of the apothecary," where the 1611 wording is, "Dead flies cause the ointment of the apothecary to send forth a stinking savor."

Not only Smith but Lancelot Andrewes and many of the other translators continued to refer to older versions for a long time. Dr. Andrewes, now Bishop of Ely, was still using an old Bible on November 1, 1617. Preaching before the king at Whitehall, he took his text—Isaiah 37:3, "The children were come to birth, and there was no strength to deliver them"—from another Bible than the one on which he had labored. He quoted an old phrasing of Deuteronomy 33:17, "With these thou shalt strike thine enemies, and push them as any wild beast." For Hebrews 12:14 he used, "Without holiness shall no man ever see God," a reading only a little off the King James. However, when he referred to Ezekiel 33:32, he really let himself go: "But all hearing (as Ezekiel complaineth) a sermon preached no otherwise than we do a ballad sung." Ezekiel's complaint in the 1611 Bible is far from that. From Revelation 14:11 Andrewes spoke of "the lake of fire and brimstone, the smoke of which shall ascend for ever more," which again is hardly a quotation.

Familiarity with the ancient texts seems to have given the translators what they regarded as a license for private interpretation; perhaps they thought in another tongue and translated as they spoke. This had long been customary with a clergy that was, as Smith said in his preface, "exercised almost from our very cradle" in Latin. And now, for the task just accomplished, they had steeped themselves in Hebrew and Greek.

But how soon did preachers begin to quote from the new version? We may say fairly that the King James Bible was in some sense a success from the start, going quickly from the two folio editions into smaller quarto and octavo sizes; yet it caught on slowly. It appears that at first both clergy and laymen found fault with the product of the learned men. Once, for instance, Dr. Richard Kilby, the translator in the Old Testament group at Oxford, heard a young parson complain in an earnest sermon that a certain passage should read in a way he stated. After the sermon Dr. Kilby took the young man aside and told him that the group had discussed at length not only his proposed reading but thirteen others; only then had they decided on the phrasing as it appeared.

Did other writers of the James I reign adopt the new Bible quickly? Robert Burton published his *Anatomy of Melancholy* in 1621, after toiling on it for years in his happy study at Christ Church, Oxford. As far as is discoverable, he never used the 1611 Bible, though he lived among some of the chief translators and had come to Christ Church through the efforts of Leonard Hutton, later a translator, then canon there. Thus Burton quoted Romans 1:21, 22: "They were vain in their imaginations, and their foolish heart was full of darkness. When they professed themselves wise, they became fools." The 1611 changes in these verses are minor but important to the style. For Job 4:18, he wrote on the same page: "Behold, he found no steadfastness in his servants, and laid folly upon his angels.' Compare with the King James verse: "Behold, he put no trust in his servants; and his angels he charged with folly." Clearly Burton was working with older Bibles, without getting around to the new version. Just as clearly, the King James reading, with its balanced rhythm, is the better.

Dr. John Donne, today thought of as poet rather than as preacher, seems to have used the King James version irregularly. In the recent edition of his sermons the first is that preached on April 30, 1615, at Greenwich, on Isaiah 52:13, which is taken from the 1611 Bible. Later in this sermon he quoted, from an early Bible, Isaiah 55:1: "Ho every one that thirsteth come to the waters, and ye that have no silver, come, buy and eat: come, I say, buy wine and milk, without silver and without money." At Paul's Cross, March 24, 1617, he made, so one wrote in a letter, "a dainty sermon." It lasted two and a half hours! There his text, Proverbs 22:11, was from the 1611 version. The now lofty translator, Archbishop Abbot, was present.

Before the king at Whitehall, April 12, 1618, Donne quoted Job 1:1 from some early Bible: "There was a man in the land of Huz, called Job, an upright and just man that feared God." At the height of his powers, Christmas Day, 1626, he preached at St. Paul's on Luke 2:29, 30, using the King James phrasing. There however he cited Isaiah 62:1 from an early Bible: "Oh that thou wouldst rend the heavens and come down." It was in this sermon that he said, "When my soul prays without any voice, my very body is then a temple." More and more he now seemed to use the 1611 Bible, for at St. Paul's on Whitsunday, 1627, though he shortened Acts 2:1–4, he gave virtually the King James wording.

How much did the King James Bible impress itself on the Plymouth Pilgrims? Three of their preachers, though they never came to Plymouth, were Henry Ainsworth, Henry Jacob, and John Robinson. There is almost nothing to show that any of them ever used the King James Bible.

Those who cut themselves off from the English Church often chose to divorce themselves from the Church Scriptures too, and to use a Bible less tainted, as it seemed to them—e.g., the Geneva—or to make their own translations, if they were capable of it. Thus Ainsworth rendered some of the Scriptures in his own way while the king's translators were working. His Psalm 23 is worth giving here. "Jehovah feedeth me, I shall not lack. In folds of budding grass he maketh me to lie down; he easily leadeth me by the waters of rests. He returneth my soul; he leadeth me in the beaten paths of justice, for his name sake. Yea, though I should walk in the valley of the shade of death, I will not fear evil, for thou wilt be with me, thy rod and thy staff they shall comfort me.

[ *139* ]

Thou furnishest before me a table in presence of my distresses; thou makest fat my head with oil; my cup is abundant. Doubtless good and mercy shall follow me all the days of my life; and I shall converse in the house of Jehovah to length of days." This was Psalm 23 as for many years the Pilgrims knew it. They had and preferred all the Psalms in Ainsworth's somewhat roughened prose. Elder William Brewster, when he died in 1644, left some of Ainsworth's books.

Henry Jacob, while in England, engaged in an intense conflict with the translator Thomas Bilson, Bishop of Winchester. Bilson he charged with "equivocation" and "most impertinent, ambiguous and uncertain writing." The origin of the dispute is obscure, but much of it was about bishops and their supposed functions. Jacob quoted Bilson as saying, "The kingdom and throne which Christ reserved for himself far passeth directing and ordering on outward things in the church which he hath left to others." Countering, Jacob said, "Nay sure, he hath not left it to others. He still reserveth this authority and dignity to himself under the gospel as well as he did under the law." To put it bluntly, how Christ governs the church must depend, so it seemed to Jacob, on what the local church, its pastor and its people decide is his will —good Congregational doctrine. We could hardly expect this kindly but determined rebel to lean on the 1611 Bible, which Bishop Bilson had helped keep within the fixed framework of the Church. On John 10:5 Jacob said with feeling, "His sheep hear his voice; a stranger's voice they will flee from." He spoke at the synod of Dort which discussed the new Bible. A few years later, about 1622, Jacob crossed the ocean to Virginia and started a pastorate of his own.

John Robinson, pastor of the Pilgrims at Leyden, and a friend of the Puritan translator Laurence Chaderton, was citing older Scriptures as late as 1625. Thus for

Psalm 41:2 he gave, "O blessed is he that prudently attendeth the poor weakling," which is far from the King James rendering. For I Timothy 3:15 he offered, "that he might know how to converse in the church of God." (To converse, remember, meant to behave.) From Robinson's sometimes piquant writings, which include many verses from the old Bibles, we get the picture of a beloved antique.

The Pilgrims, among them remnants of the Brownists, were almost as much against the Puritans as they were against the high churchmen and the papists. So they were slow, it appears, to accept the King James Bible, put out by those who had harassed them. In the long run the 1611 Bible, because of its stature, triumphed with the Pilgrims as with their old foes, except those in the Church of Rome, and to it they referred all details of daily living.

In England too, acceptance of the new Bible was to depend on the climate of controversy. That was changing, and eventually the King James version would become a frame of reference to be cited as authority. But at the start it partook of the personal controversies and associations of the translators themselves, and so roused opposition. The old Arminian bitterness was not forgotten, though now, under Bancroft, the state Church had been leaning somewhat toward Arminian doctrines. The beliefs of Calvin that God had destined all events, great and small, were giving way a little to the belief that God destined only in part, with good works of value along with the faith of the elect. It was argued that Calvin's predestination, so valuable to the Puritans because it freed man from the tyranny of Rome, made God the author of sin and gave false security to those who believed themselves the elect. Besides "Dutch" Thomson, many of the translators, among them Overall, Bois, and Richardson, were counted on the Arminian side. Laurence Chaderton and young Samuel Ward were of the opposition and

Bishop Abbot stood firmly opposed; no Arminian could ever appease him. But the king, who spoke out against Arminians abroad, endured them and was even pleasant to them at home. A joke of the time asked, What do the Arminians hold? The answer was, they hold the best deaneries and bishoprics in England.

Other dissenters still had their troubles. From the Arian heresy evolved, after a long time, the Unitarians. Yet the Church felt it must kill the first of these heretics to speak out in the time of James, without objection from the king who had promised no bloodshed over religion.

Bartholomew Legate, already mentioned, was one who believed that Jesus was a mere man, that there was no virgin birth, no Incarnation. When he preached this belief, both George Abbot and Lancelot Andrewes of the translators approved his sentence to death. Abbot indeed wrote a letter to Lord Ellesmere, the Lord Chancellor, saying that the king "did not much desire that the Lord Coke should be called" to the trial, "lest by his singularity in opinion he should give stay to the business." There was no stay; the trial moved to its ruthless end. In Smithfield Market on March 18, 1611, at the urging of Andrewes, Abbot, and other firmly irate divines, the king's agents burned Bartholomew Legate at the stake.

A few days later on March 24, the seventh anniversary of James's accession, Andrewes—now Bishop of Ely—preached before the king at Whitehall. Through times that had been enough to disturb him to the utmost, he had kept his pious bearing. His text was Psalm 118:22–24, "This is the Lord's day; it is marvelous in our eyes"— a verse he had used previously for thanksgiving after discovery of the Guy Fawkes plot. "This stone is the head," Andrewes declared, meaning the king, "made by God." Words spoken in hope, surely, for the last few months must have been for Andrewes a time of most earnest prayer and legitimate expectation.

Before Christmas the great bell at St. Paul's had tolled the news that the see of Canterbury was once more vacant. Richard Bancroft died November 10, 1610, before he could hold in his hands the printed Bible he had first opposed at Hampton Court, then had taken under his charge to please the king. Many of the clergy and the people thought with pleasure that at last Lancelot Andrewes, who had a living odor of sainthood, would rise to the summit.

Ever since the death of Archbishop Whitgift in 1604 and the choice of Bancroft for the great place, Andrewes must have worked with quiet hope in his sermons, in all his acts during those years, and his patient work on the Bible. Though John Bois, Miles Smith, and many others had worked harder on the translation than Andrewes, they were minor figures in the Church, compared with him. The supreme gift of the king could rightly reward his faith and good works as a prelate. Among God's elect he clearly deserved the chief crown of the righteous or rightly wise, and a long life of power.

King James delayed. True, Andrewes was among the highest of the high churchmen, and had many potent friends. The king loved his preaching. But on the other hand James, a Scotsman, thought of the Scots. On October 21, 1610, Lancelot Andrewes, George Abbot, and two other bishops had consecrated in the chapel of a London house three bishops of Scotland, the first thus to receive holy sanction from the Church of England. Bishop Abbot had wholly sympathized with the king's haste to see the Scottish Church established, which he understood as clearly as he had understood the royal desire for a speedy end to Bartholomew Legate. In Legate's burning Andrewes had concurred, but now he balked somewhat at the royal will. The difficulty was that the new Scottish prelates were men of low degree in the Church, as none were eligible for such advancement. Abbot, a practical man, saw no harm in their rapid elevation. But Lancelot Andrewes, though he participated in the ceremony, let it be known that he felt it to be unseemly.

Now there were months of suspense about Andrewes' own advancement, during which he must have composed some of his most fervent daily prayers. Translated from the Latin he used, these private devotions exist today in his published works.

At length on March 18, just before the burning of Bartholomew Legate, the king made his choice. To succeed Richard Bancroft he picked a man whom none had backed in the open—not the learned Bishop of Ely, but the Bishop of London, prosy George Abbot. Abbot himself said that he was wonder-struck.

George Abbot thus arrived at enough success for anyone. On his knees in sincere thankfulness—for he cannot have taken seriously the story about his mother and the pike—he must have been sure that God and the word of God, newly rendered, had impelled him on to the goal.

Installed by proxy May 16, 1611, a month after he had begun to live at Lambeth, Archbishop Abbot threw himself with vigor into the varied doings of his office. While his preferment amazed and depressed the Anglicans, the Puritans, to whom he was friendly, tried to conceal their happy hopes. At the court the king was cordial, and even the queen, though in secret a papist with no use for him, deigned to speak to him with a polite show. Soon he took his seat on the privy council. James desired him to be lavish with social life at Lambeth Palace. His income from the Church made him one of the richest men in England, able to live in grandeur amid the music, the colors, the forms which the best English talent contrived. Within his realm he could command service proper for his high estate, could exert power and enjoy feeling power, in designs that he had long craved as the most noble on earth. In his day this sullen translator with a Puritan bent, now the highest prelate in Great Britain, had become the most famous of all the learned men.

The new archbishop was honest and a hard worker. He tended to be a low churchman where Lancelot Andrewes, that more gracious translator, would have been high, and where James himself might have preferred stricter forms. An odd man to follow Richard Bancroft, Abbot felt bound to lead, and he did have some measure of leadership in his narrow, crabbed make-up. Yet one of his lacks was that he had never held a post in which he had to concern himself with the care of souls. Out of touch with the common people, he was often tactless and stupid. With little zeal for or skill in preaching, he was born just to have views, to manage, and to command. He was a great one to reprove, and though tender to the scruples of the Puritans, he maintained that all should comply with the forms of worship enjoined by the law of the land. With all his scowls he was deeply pious and never flinched in his duty, which he knew to be a light to guide and a rod to check the erring.

Abbot's gain of the highest church post and Legate's loss of his life marked the year of publication of the King James Bible, and characterized the England that received it. Abbot's elevation probably helped the new version along, as Andrewes' would have done. Legate's fate suggests that it was needed. And Miles Smith's preface, though he began like an Elizabethan playwright with an apology to the reader, really meant not to apologize but to reprove the world he addressed.

"Zeal to promote the common good," Smith began, "whether it be by devising anything ourselves, or revising that which hath been labored by others, deserveth certainly much respect and esteem, but yet findeth but cold entertainment in the world." (Note the use of "devising" and "revising" in the manner of Lyly.) "It is welcomed with suspicion instead of with love. . . . For was there ever any thing projected, that savored any way of newness or renewing, but the same endured many a storm of gain-saying, or opposition? A man would think that civility, wholesome laws, learning and eloquence, synods and church maintenance (that we speak of no more things of this kind) should be as safe as a sanctuary, and out of shot, as they say, that no man would lift up the heel, no, nor dog move his tongue against the motioners of them." Yet, rather, Smith went on, "He that meddleth with men's religion in any part meddleth with their custom, nay, with their freehold: and though they can find no content in that which they have, yet they cannot abide to hear of any altering. . . ."

And so, at the end of the great Bible task, Smith sadly but bravely anticipated opposition. "If we will be sons of the truth, we must consider that it speaketh, and trample upon our own credit, yea, and upon other men's too, if either be in any way a hindrance."

Happily, the royal command at Hampton Court could give the new version enough prestige to insure its adoption, in time, by all the churchmen loyal to the Crown. Other authorization there was none, although like the Bishops' Bible of 1585 the new Bible called itself "Authorized" and "Appointed to be read in churches." How that came about is uncertain; perhaps the phrase was merely picked up from the old title page. And so, although there is no record that Abbot, Bancroft before him, or any with power to do so ever "authorized" the King James Bible, people speak of it as the Authorized Version.

Although the new Bible could supplant the Bishops' Bible in the churches (the latter was not reprinted after 1611), it was at first too big a volume for daily household use. It could spread widely among the people only when, in the octavo edition of 1612, it became small enough to be read by the fireside, held in the hand instead of resting on a table. For fires were still used for lights in English cottages, as well as for burning dissenters in the market place.

More, people—such people as thronged Smithfield to watch Bartholomew Legate burned—had to learn to read. Presumably the first *common* people to read the new Bible were the nameless workers in Robert Barker's print shop who put it through the press. There, at the sign of the Tiger's Head, they ably abetted the men who were learned in tongues. All wrought with their minds and their hands to perfect for us the work, approved unto God, rightly setting forth the word of truth.

# CHAPTER 14

# Rewards and Sequels

All of the learned men, each in his degree, had some worldly success. What writers of the age outside the Church could be certain of plenty to live on? God supplied His own with what they needed. In that faith, the learned men were secure as they sought their stipends from those in charge of sacred administration. On the whole they lived in sedate order, fitting for their weighty work.

Giles Thomson, for instance, who had been Dean of Windsor, became Bishop of Gloucester in 1611 before the Bible came out. But he never got even to visit his see; within a year he died.

On September 20, 1616, Miles Smith succeeded Thomson as Bishop of Gloucester, being ordained to that office at Croydon, then just outside London but now part of the city. Archbishop Abbot must have had much to do with this reward for Miles Smith, which was, they said, mainly for his writing the preface to the improved Bible.

Gloucester is in the west of England, farther from London than many other sees. It was, one might think, a sort of safe refuge. The church needed repairs, which Smith was slow in making. One of his chief concerns was to keep the table for the Lord's Supper lengthwise in the nave, instead of crosswise before the altar; for the latter arrangement was seen as a symbol stressing the real presence, the belief that the body and blood of Christ Jesus are in the bread and wine, a concept from which the Puritans shied away. We can understand why people contended about the placing of the table only as we see that the Puritans deemed the doctrine of the real presence popish and were staunchly against it. The High Church of England, on the other hand, wished in many ways to approach the Church of Rome and yet remain itself.

At Westminster Abbey, Archbishop Abbot was making changes that seemed Puritan. He refused bowing at the altar and at the name of Christ. The choir, the organ, and the cope went slowly into disuse. The whole service was now so simple that it could have pleased Calvin. Prelates verging on the Puritan, such as Abbot and Smith, doubted the need for bishops, and yet were eager enough to be bishops themselves. There were many rumbles before the lashing storm to come. If the Puritans were gaining strength, so was the High Church of England.

Soon a rising man named William Laud became Dean of Gloucester, determined to oppose each Puritan practice of Bishop Smith. Others than Abbot must have advised the king to send Laud there. In 1616 Laud, always ruthless, went straight against the dictates of Smith, put the table again before the altar, restored the cope and the bowings, and made the service at Gloucester high enough to express his almost popish aims. As dean, he had power to order all this. Abbot and Smith both despised Laud and his changes, which restored the dearest trappings of priesthood. However, as Laud had the ear of the king, formal counter orders would have been highly unwise.

Bishop Smith left the great church buildings in dudgeon, and declared that he would stay away until Laud removed the hated symbols. The town was in an uproar. Most of the people were for Bishop Smith. They met and marched in the streets, in effect picketing Laud and what was to them wicked nonsense. Yet the ascent of Laud was rapid and sure. The people and their bishop in due course had to give up their revolt, which now appeared hopeless. They suppressed their outward disdain, because the Church was still theirs to love. It might have been some comfort to them if they could have known, as we know today, how Laud was at length to fall.

Just now in Gloucester any prospect of his fall was remote. Miles Smith, who was getting on in years, had to smother much of his chagrin. Through his trials, his sermons show, his own virtue gave him a secret gladness. His joy that he was a Puritan, and therefore right, no man could take from him.

A private quarrel at this time disrupted a long friendship between two of the translators, both good men and whole-hearted scholars. At the time they worked together at Stationers' Hall, Andrew Downes and John Bois were also aiding their associate Sir Henry Savile in his mammoth eight-volume edition of St. Chrysostom. How could they undertake so much work? Here is a measure of their scholarship and energy, but overexertion may have affected their tempers. Unhappily, they fell into intense conflict over the greater credit that Sir Henry Savile seemed, to Downes, to give to Bois for their help on the whalelike private opus.

The Bois and Downes notes on St. Chrysostom are all in Latin and Greek. Judging from the writing, there are as many by the one as by the other. They extend to scores of pages. Savile seems to have been fair in giving credit to both. Sometimes he wrote *non probo,* I do not prove, beside some comment by one or the other of his helpers. Downes grew so jealous that he stopped speaking to his former pupil, while the milder Bois went on praising his former teacher. In his smallness the zeal of the Lord turned inward and almost consumed Downes. Fortunately the break between them came after the two had finished their nine months' work at Stationers' Hall.

Savile and Downes, too, became wholly estranged. On

the other hand, Savile and Bois remained friends. Once when Sir Henry lay sick, Lady Savile said that if he died, she would burn Chrysostom for killing her husband. Bois replied that Chrysostom was one of the sweetest preachers since the apostles, and so satisfied her that she said she would not do it for all the world. Sir Henry survived. But now the whole massive eight volumes of Savile's St. Chrysostom are dead upon the shelves that hold rare books, while the superb Bible to which Bois, Downes, and Savile gave their best efforts lives on.

Meanwhile, Archbishop Abbot, because of his office, had to mingle more than any other translator in events that concerned the nation. Streaming tears, he sat by the bed of young Henry, Prince of Wales, who died of cold and fever on November 6, 1612. His prayer at the deathbed was "most exceeding powerful, passionate." Then he preached at the burial service in Westminster Abbey. Next he married the Princess Elizabeth to the Elector Palatine, on February 12, 1613. Thus, so one writer praised God a hundred years ago, began the line which brought to Great Britain the blessing of good Queen Victoria.

Abbot could be fulsome about the king, with whom he was often at odds. The life of King James, he said, "hath been so immaculate and unspotted in the world, so free from all touch of viciousness and staining imputation, that even malice itself, which leaveth nothing unsearched, could never find true blemish in it, nor cast probably aspersion on it. . . . All must acknowledge him to be zealous as David, learned and wise, the Solomon of our age, religious as Josiah, careful of spreading Christ's faith as Constantine the great, just as Moses, undefiled in all his ways as Jehoshaphat, or Hezekiah, full of clemency as another Theodosius." Such pratings were just churchly eyewash, wholly absurd.

Troubles piled up for the archbishop. Frances Howard, Countess of Essex, was suing to void her marriage. At thirteen she had married the Earl of Essex, then fourteen, son of the Essex whose head Queen Elizabeth had ordered cut off. It had been a foolish marriage followed by ten years of contention and falling away from grace. Now the countess, doubtless goaded on by King James himself, was nerving herself to marry Robert Carr, Viscount Rochester, new Earl of Somerset, a former page whom the king had quickly pushed forward. The case was messy and Archbishop Abbot found himself in the thick of it.

As one of the group named to adjudge the merits of the pleas, Abbot, staying with the king at Windsor, fell on his knees and begged release. Most writers have called this the case of the Essex divorce. It was rather a suit to annul the marriage. Both Church and state had to deal with it. Abbot was honest enough to declare his qualms; the king induced him to go on seeking the facts, but as it were, packed the court by adding to it some of whom he was sure. The chief of these was Thomas Bilson, Bishop of Winchester, Miles Smith's associate in the final draft of the Bible.

Always Bilson was discreet in being for the High Church. He remained so now. What seemed to be a simple case of divorce was clearly for the Church to oppose, but Bilson knew which side his bread was buttered on. Abbot's dislike for him grew intense. The discord between them, though less open, was greater than that between those other translators, John Bois and Andrew Downes. Downes was merely jealous of Bois because Bois seemed to get more credit than he for the work both did for Sir Henry Savile. Abbot was averse to Bilson because of wholly opposed viewpoints. Low where Bilson was high, Abbot was still a good enough churchman to deplore any semblance of divorce, which the Church had to condemn.

Many a witness gave vivid evidence, all damning to the earl, though he was merely a helpless wight. Plainly he and his wife wanted to quit each other. In his brave survey of the case, Abbot said among other things, "Inasmuch as we firmly believe that the Scripture doth directly or by consequence contain in it sufficient matter to decide all controversies, especially in all things appertaining to the church, as that marriage among Christians can be no less accounted than a sacred thing . . . I would be glad to know, and by what text of Scripture, either by the old or new testament, a man may have a warrant to make a nullity of a marriage solemnly celebrated."

King James answered in person: "That the Scripture doth directly or by consequence contain sufficient matter to decide all controversies, especially in this appertaining to the church: This in my opinion is preposterous, and one of the Puritans' arguments, without a better distinction of application." Abbot, by the way, quoted Matthew 19:12 from an old Bible, though he had helped translate that very passage in the new Bible. Then, with courage to stand against the king, Abbot voted against the dissolution of the marriage. The toady translator, Bishop Thomas Bilson, voted yes, and with others of like mind, prevailed, seven to six. King James had insured the verdict.

The countess, freed from Essex, soon married Carr. There followed a further scandal. Young Sir Thomas Overbury, a crude poet, had helped Carr and the countess during their intrigue, but had balked at the thought of their being husband and wife. So the hapless poet got sent to the Tower. There he languished and, in extreme pain, died. In time Lady Somerset confessed that she had connived to bring about his death, as a tool now turned against her and her new husband. The first poisoned fruit tarts went astray. Then the keeper, at the instance of a drug man whom the Somersets had secured, fed Sir Thomas white arsenic; *aqua fortis*, which is nitric acid; mercury; powder of diamonds; *lapis causticus;* great spiders; and cantharides, which are dried beetles or Spanish flies. All these worked slowly. At the end the keeper gave the doomed man a clyster of corrosive sublimate. During the trial King James brought up the subject of witchcraft, largely to show off his crafty power to reason. Four were put to death for the crime. James at length pardoned the Earl and Countess of Somerset, who left the court to become misty figures in the background of the time.

Honest Archbishop Abbot felt sorely troubled about his failure to prevent all this. Yet he was full of notions of his own. He brought in, to replace Carr in the king's favor, young George Villiers, who got out of the prelate's hand, and rose quickly to be Duke of Buckingham. The duke's story is beyond our range, but in time all who wanted to promote any schemes and to get on in the Stuart world had to bribe this flaunting upstart. Such doings reflect the social tone of the times through which the 1611 Bible had to make its way.

Nevertheless the King James Bible began to seep into common living. First it made progress in the churches, where the clergy here and there preached from it. Listeners took to heart and treasured certain verses, sometimes because they were novel and striking, sometimes because they were apt and fluent. Then the new Bible found its way into some homes for reading, for learning to read, and for times of prayer. More careful study evolved by degrees, until the phrasings passed into daily language. This progress can be traced through writings of the Stuart period.

Effects of the revised Bible on conduct, in accordance with Abbot's plea that the Scriptures could answer all controversies, are harder to trace. Many have argued that it had an appreciable effect on English morality. At any rate the common people came to depend on it for stricter guidance.

Amid more rewards for the learned men, there were

more deaths too, as if their labors on the Bible had been too much. Dr. John Aglionby had died in the prime of life while the Bible was in the press. When an older translator, Dr. Thomas Holland, died, a fellow translator, Dr. Richard Kilby, preached his funeral sermon at St. Mary's, Oxford. Among others who died in these first few years after 1611 were John Harmer, Warden of St. Mary's College; George Ravis, Warden of New College; John Spenser, who had succeeded Rainolds as president of Corpus Christi College, Oxford; and Richard Thomson, the fat-bellied Arminian, who, they said, went to bed drunk each night. The only translator who is known to have traveled abroad after 1611 was William Bedwell; in 1612 he journeyed to Leyden to see Scaliger's Arabian books and papers.

In 1614 John Overall, Dean of St. Paul's, the translator whose wife ran away only to return under duress, became Bishop of Lichfield and Coventry. William Barlow, who had been at the Hampton Court meeting and had written up that conclave, and who had worked hard on the Bible, now rose to be Bishop of Lincoln, after having had the least see of Rochester. Bishop Lancelot Andrewes made worthy John Bois, who left us his painful notes, a prebend of Ely—a reward that seems tiny for his minute toil.

Then on June 16, 1616, died the Bishop of Winchester, Thomas Bilson. His long service to the king, rather than his work with Miles Smith on the final Bible draft, made it seem fitting to bury him in Westminster Abbey. Bilson's death left one of the best sees in England open for a good man. Lancelot Andrewes, we recall, had hoped to be primate after Bancroft died but had lost out to Abbot. At length, doubtless approved by Low Church Abbot, this high churchman who got along well with all became Bishop of Winchester. More and more he used the 1611 Bible in his sermons.

Others who died in this period were Jeremy Radcliffe;

John Perin, Canon of Christ Church, Oxford; Dr. Ralph Ravens, Dean of Wells; and Dr. John Duport, Vice-Chancellor of Cambridge. On November 6, 1617, died Dr. John Layfield, the translator who had gone on a voyage to the West Indies and written an Elizabethan account of it. Long Rector of St. Clement Danes in London, the famous church later associated with Dr. Samuel Johnson, Layfield had just repaired the steeple.

The next year John Overall, Bishop of Lichfield and Coventry, rose a few notches to be Bishop of Norwich, where the Puritans had been strong but where he leaned toward Arminianism. Within a year he too was dead. While the Pilgrims were landing on Cape Cod, on November 7, 1620, Dr. Richard Kilby, Rector of Lincoln College, Oxford, died at sixty.

Like most Puritans, Archbishop Abbot believed in strict keeping of the Sabbath. In 1618 the king issued an edict in which he approved of sports on Sunday after all the sacred duties had been observed. Abbot, who was staying at Croydon, forbade the reading of this edict in the parish church there. Trying to live in accordance with the Bible, he knew that God Himself rested on the seventh day, surely without turning to games. In after years Abbot was to speak of James I as "my master," yet he was often fearless to oppose the king.

Even after showing his disapproval of the edict about Sabbath sports, Archbishop Abbot remained enough in favor to preach at the funeral service for Queen Anne on March 13, 1619. And he had gone on with his lesser duties, such as keeping an eye on All Souls College, Oxford. "I do require you, Mr. Warden, and the rest of the officers," he wrote, "severally to punish such as in your society are neglecting their studies to spend their time abroad in taverns and ale houses to the defamation of scholars and scandal of your house, and not to impart any common favors unto them unless they thoroughly reform themselves." In those lax days the maligned, serious archbishop could seem a nuisance to roistering youth.

For his home town of Guildford, Abbot had founded and endowed a sort of rest home. In it he reserved rooms for his own use. Much later John Evelyn in his diary wrote of a visit to this hospice. Abbot, of course, was now getting richer and grander in his own eyes. Two of his brothers, one a member of the East India Company and of the Council of New England, the other about to become Bishop of Salisbury, prospered along with him. The archbishop was at the height of a career which the seeress had promised his mother would come of her eating a young pike.

At midsummer, 1621, Edward Zouche, eleventh baron of that name and Warden of the Cinque Ports, a high office in the state, invited the primate to his great, formal house and spreading park at Bramshill in Hampshire. On July 24, not the Sabbath but a Tuesday, Lord Zouche and his party went deer hunting. The stout, stuffy archbishop wanted to be manful with the bow and arrow, but was a poor shot. Time after time he warned the men who were beating up the game to keep back a goodly distance. Eager to please His Grace by chasing at least one deer within bow cast of him, they were reckless. A buck came into sight. Abbot twanged his bow. His arrow —and arrows in those days were sharp, deadly weapons —hit one of the keepers in the arm. Blood gushed out and before long poor Peter Harkins had bled to death. Thus George Abbot became the only translator of the 1611 Bible and the only Archbishop of Canterbury ever to kill a human being.

Abbot was in an abyss of grief, stabbed with the sternest feelings of guilt. At once he retired to his new hospice at Guildford. On the widow he settled twenty pounds a year, which gave her the means to shorten her mourning and quickly get a second husband. The Church and the court seethed with dismay and censure. What right had the primate of the English Church to go hunting?

No canon in the English Church forbade a bishop's taking part in field sports. Indeed, so to take part was a portion of the Episcopal right. Queen Elizabeth's Archbishop Whitgift had once killed twenty bucks. The Bible said nothing about stag hunting. King James had charged Abbot that he should carry his house nobly and live like an archbishop, which the prelate had promised him to do.

The case was one for church decision, and a group including Bishop Lancelot Andrewes met for long searching and debate. It even referred the matter on the side to the Sorbonne at Paris. Had Abbot become "irregular" and "incapable by common law of discharging his duties"?

Meanwhile friends of Abbot were cool to him, and foes cast slurs at him when he dared to preach in the country. Yet in September he went briefly to the court again, where the king put himself out to be kind. Lancelot Andrewes quibbled and wavered as he sought to placate all, and the judgment when reached was rather vague, but in sum absolved Abbot, with Andrewes more or less for him. The Sorbonne seemed, in the main, against him. On December 24 the king deemed it best to proclaim a formal pardon. By law the primate's private estate was forfeit to the Crown. But James said: "An angel might have miscarried in this sort. . . . The king would not add affliction to his sorrow or take one farthing from his chattels and movables."

Though thus affirmed in his office, Abbot found the respect of many people waning. He could do nothing to allay a persistent feeling that a primate who killed a man was less holy than he should be. His high power, which he was still keen to assert, subtly lessened. The rest of his long service teemed with his crotchets, his temper, his rather futile judgments, and the efforts of high churchmen to subdue him. Laud, now a bishop, he rightly thought one of his chief stumbling blocks, though for the present Laud knew how to avoid too blatant outbursts.

Sir Henry Savile, the most handsome of the translators, died at Eton on February 19, 1622. They buried him by torchlight to save expense, though he left two hundred pounds for the rites. The useful Miles Smith, Bishop of Gloucester, died October 20, 1624, after forlorn last years of conformity to practices he disliked.

On February 14, 1625, was buried at Wilden, Bedfordshire, Francis Dillingham, the bachelor translator who knew how a man could be happy though married by keeping his wife subject to him. The translator Dr. John Richardson, Master of Peterhouse, died April 20, 1626, leaving one hundred pounds to build a brick wall in front of the college next to the street. That same year the translator Robert Spalding slept with his fathers. Most accounts of the lives of all these men marked the fact that they had helped translate the King James Bible. For that work their own world rightly honored them as true scholars of the first rank.

Amid the deaths and honors the king had been ever intent on money. "My lords," he had said in 1619 to two bishops, Neale of Durham and Andrewes of Winchester, "cannot I take my subjects' money when I want it without all this formality in parliament?" The two bishops were standing behind his chair at dinner. Neale said, "You should; you are the breath of our nostrils." Lancelot Andrewes said that he had "no skill in parliamentary cases," but, "I think it lawful for you to take my brother Neale's money, because he offers it." The king's concern for money was always grasping. As his reign lengthened the nation endured him without conceiving that there might be worse to come.

The profound event of 1625 was the death of King James on March 27, after ten days of illness. Four days before the end he, or perhaps those around him, sent for Archbishop Abbot, who gave the dying man extreme unction after the way of the English Church. Someone else conducted the final service to bury the wise old fool.

The coming of Charles I to the throne increased the partial eclipse of Abbot. Laud, called in from St. David's, Wales, where he was bishop, and before long made Bishop of London, was moving steadily upward. The marriage of the new king to Henrietta Maria of France was by proxy. The crowning, court and Church said, had to be on a holy feast day. This one they at length set for Candlemas, the purification day of St. Mary the Virgin, February 2, 1626, nearly a year after the death of James.

Having long suffered from gout, the stone, and gravel, all no doubt due in part to high living, Abbot aroused himself. Four new bishops had refused with good conscience to have him install them. He was a tainted primate. Yet before the great day he, with others, revised the order for the supreme pageant of coronation. The plague had once more been rife. By royal command, Archbishop Abbot, Bishop Lancelot Andrewes, and others consulted on a form of thanks to God that the plague was getting less. On the splendid day itself, Abbot was later to complain and boast, the archbishop "had work enough for the strongest man in England." That was true, as we know from the crowning of Queen Elizabeth II.

The drama was much the same then as now. There were exact plans for the crowning of Queen Henrietta Maria, too, with a chair or throne set out for her. Queen Anne before her had refused to take the oath in the Church of England, but was present in silence throughout the ordeal. Now Henrietta Maria, with papist firmness, stayed away but watched the whole pomp from a vantage point built for her. As the hours went by, other observers saw with horror the queen's ladies dancing and frisking; Stuart youth was sportive and Charles was only twenty-five.

On the morning of February 2, the monarch of all he surveyed went to Westminster Abbey by water. Abbot and the others had, of course, received the order of the day in advance and knew just what to do. The almost Puritan archbishop, in a cope of gold brocade which must have weighed down his shoulders and perhaps his conscience, too, spoke to the people in due form. Then he received the king at the altar which bore a High Church cross. There were the traditional questions to the king and the king's formal answers. Then the archbishop had to anoint the royal body. He took the jeweled crown of King Edward in his hands, laid it before the king on the altar, and offered the prayer. He put the ring on the fourth finger of the king's right hand, gave him the scepter and the rod, and enthroned him.

Bending his gouty joints and kneeling, he declared, "I, George Abbot, shall be faithful." The Scripture reading, still from some older Bible, was I Peter 2:11–13: "Dearly beloved, I beseech you as strangers and pilgrims to abstain from fleshly lusts, which fight against the soul, and see that you have honest conversation among the Gentiles, that whereas they backbite you as evil doers, they may see your good works and praise God in the day of visitation." Those pointed verses must have sounded like Puritan warnings, for in the months before the crowning, religious strife had been waxing more acrid.

Now the archbishop gave the king Holy Communion. Charles sat down in King Edward's chair. The archbishop lifted the heavy crown and put it on the king's head, saying, "God crown thee with a crown of glory and righteousness." The lords and ladies donned their coronets. It was done.

The whole display of regal gleaming was much longer than this brief account implies. Abbot, the only one of the Bible translators who crowned a king of England, went through it all well. It was, as always, a brilliant, awesome scene. The robes had plenty of crimson and purple. The young king was a fresh hope for the people. Or was he? Archbishop Abbot seemed to submerge any hope he may have had in his wonted sad sourness. Yet as he ached and glowered, he was oddly more vital than the show around him, because he knew that the word of our God shall stand forever.

Then the bells pealed and the people shouted, the horses pranced and the royal coach rolled along with the king being gracious. Thus with an archbishop who favored the Puritans and bishops who were of the High Church, began a reign which was to be one of ever-raging conflicts and to have a brutal, lurid end on the scaffold.

Slowly thereafter Abbot sank out of general view. Sometimes others carried him into the House of Lords, where he spoke from a chair. In the House of Commons his friend Sir Dudley Digges, whom he had tutored at University College, Oxford, and others looked upon him as a bulwark against Bishop William Laud, recognized as an enemy, and also against George Villiers, Duke of Buckingham, whose rise he had at first mistakenly supported. Now against the dangerous favorite Abbot wrote a long defense of himself: "The duke of Buckingham (being still great in the favor of the king, could endure no man that would not depend upon him) among others had me in his eye, for not stooping unto him, so as to become his vassal." From an old Bible he quoted Psalm 112:7: "He shall not be afraid of any evil tidings, for his heart standeth fast, and believeth in the Lord." Thus fifteen years after he finished work on the 1611 Bible he refrained from citing it.

In 1627 he had so far fallen from the king's good will that they tried to relieve him of his duties and take away his office. He had bitter words for those who thus attacked him. "In the courts of princes there is little feeling for the infirmities belonging to old age. They like them that be young, and gallant in their actions, and in their clothes. They love not that any man should stick too long in any room of greatness." No translator of the 1611 Bible, and least of all George Abbot, Archbishop of Canterbury, should have had to say that. Of himself he said: "I cannot deny that the indisposition of my body kept me from court and therefore gave occasion to maligners to traduce me." At last they set him apart, "sequestered" him. William Laud, Bishop of London, assumed many of the prelate's tasks. For him and his almost papist stand Charles had taken a strong liking.

In the meantime even gracious, smiling Bishop Lancelot Andrewes of Winchester had died, September 26, 1626. John Milton, aged seventeen, at once wrote a stiff Latin paean at Christ's College, Cambridge. As Andrewes entered heaven, "Each angel saluted his new comrade with embrace and song, and from the placid lips of One came these words: 'Come, son, enjoy the gladness of thy Father's realm; rest henceforth from thy hard labors.' As He spoke, the winged choirs touched their psalteries." Later Milton was to write against this same gentle bishop in the old dispute over episcopal power in the Church.

While Laud enlarged his scope, the Puritans fought their way forward. The 1611 Bible by its own worth was making itself welcome throughout the country, for those on both sides needed the best modern texts with which to fight their doctrinal skirmishes. High churchmen in greater numbers began to use the 1611 version, which in centuries to come would be the sole bond uniting the countless English-speaking Protestant sects.

In 1629 the Bible was again revised, but only in small ways, and once more in minor respects in 1638. The last issue of the Geneva Bible was in 1644. By then the King James version was ahead of all others, and now the strife over forms and doctrine helped it on.

"The gospel," Puritan Sir John Eliot had burst forth

in the House of Commons, "is that truth in which his kingdom has been happy. . . . That truth, not with words but with actions, we will maintain." In their worst hours the Puritans "turned to the new world to redress the balance of the old." Many of them now founded Boston, where they used the Bible as a book of ground rules.

The learned men had all come of age before 1604, and so were to die before most of their Plymouth brethren and the Puritans in America. Andrew Downes had died in 1628, still full of rancor against his former pupil and colleague in the Bible work, John Bois. Jeffrey King, the translator who had held the royal chair of Hebrew at Oxford, died in 1630. Other translators who soon died were Roger Andrewes, Master of Jesus College, who had made his progress through the help of his brother Lancelot, and Thomas Harrison, Puritan, who had been vice-prefect of Trinity College, Cambridge. Leonard Hutton died May 17, 1632, aged seventy-five, and went to his last rest in Christ Church.

While "sequestered" in 1627, Archbishop Abbot was still fasting each Tuesday in sorrow for his killing of the gamekeeper years before. He had days of being better and days of being worse, but his power in Church and state was about gone. At last Abbot died at Croydon, August 4, 1633, aged seventy-one. He had served twenty-one years, three times as long as Bancroft. In after years his opponents would say that his service was "fatal' to the Church of England, a statement hardly exact, since the Church of England remains lively. Unknowingly kindling the flames of conflict which at length broke out in the great revolt, Abbot deemed Christian only that which abhorred and reviled papal forms. On the whole he valued men in accordance with their zeal for antipopery. His house was an isle of safety for the foremost in the factious party of the Church, whose writings he licensed, and he relaxed penal laws against them. Thus he gave courage to future rebels who were, years after, to get rid of both Laud and King Charles. At the bottom of his heart Abbot was far more a Bible scholar than a churchman. Of the translators, he played by far the most influential role in the troublous times after 1611, and his bias led in the end toward a revolution bound to come. We must give stolid George Abbot his due.

To succeed him, King Charles of course chose William Laud, Bishop of London. The new archbishop set to work putting back the emblems of the High Church. Laud had resolved to raise the Church of England as a branch, though a reformed branch, of the Church of Rome, which was thriving elsewhere. First he determined to sever such ties as had joined his church to the reformed churches of Europe. With his power as archbishop he withdrew freedom of worship from those of France and Flanders who had sought refuge in England, until crowds of them sailed from southern ports to Holland. He and his followers even forbade British soldiers and merchants abroad to attend churches which adhered to the teachings of Calvin. Passive support of the Crown, in the Church as elsewhere, was to take the place of gospel preaching.

For more of the learned men, death shortened the strain of troublous times. Richard Brett died April 15, 1637, aged seventy. His stone at Quanton, Buckinghamshire, shows him, his widow and his four daughters, all kneeling.

Now only four of the learned men were still living. Of these, one had been the youngest—Samuel Ward, Puritan, Warden of Sidney-Sussex College, who as a poor student had condemned himself for eating too many damson plums and too much cheese.

Another was Laurence Chaderton, one of the four Puritans at the Hampton Court parley. A fine old fellow with a head of gray hair, he could read without glasses when he was over a hundred. Even then he never said a thing twice as he conversed or told his harmless stories. His wife had died after they had been married fifty-five years, and his daughter had taken care of him. He died November 13, 1640, aged one hundred and three. Longer than the rest, he escaped that haunting last chapter of Ecclesiastes which he helped translate.

When Chaderton and Ward were gone, there were two left. Of these, one was John Bois. Careful in all matters, as with words, he had told four bishops of Ely that his scruples would not let him baptize a stray child that was too old to be an infant, and too young to profess any faith. In his old age he could recall details of what he had known, felt, and done, and had all his wits about him. His sight was quick, his hearing acute, his face fresh, and his skin like parchment without wrinkles. He told his children and others that if at any time he expressed any thought which savored of bad temper, they should tell him of it. The day before he died he asked that those around him move him to the room where his wife had expired—his dear, adverse, spendthrift wife, who had made him almost bankrupt. He died January 14, 1643, aged eighty-three.

So at last we come to the sole translator who, after Laud and Charles I had laid their perverse heads on the executioner's block, lived on into the rule of Cromwell. The tall, smiling Bing, who for forty-six years had been subdean at York, died at Winterton in Norfolk in March, 1652, aged seventy-eight. With Edward Lively's group, which contained among others Dillingham and Chaderton, he had helped revise the Old Testament books from I Chronicles through Job, the Psalms, the Proverbs, Ecclesiastes, and the Song of Songs. Who knows, perhaps he gave us "If I make my bed in hell, behold, Thou art there," and "Many waters cannot quench love."

# CHAPTER 15

# The Bible of the
# Learned Men Lasts

Can a committee produce a work of art? Many would say no, yet we have seen that this large group of the king's translators, almost threescore of them, together gave the world a work greater not only in scope but in excellence than any could have done singly. How did this come to be? How explain that sixty or more men, none a genius, none even as great a writer as Marlowe or Ben Jonson, together produced writing to be compared with (and confused with) the words of Shakespeare?

Group writing of various kinds has long been useful or profitable. Encyclopedists have contributed vastly to education, even to political progress. We have had successful works of pooled information, such as the guidebooks compiled by the WPA writers in the depression years. Popular movies and mysteries are written by writing "teams." The daily newspaper is an example of collective effort by scores of anonymous writers. But art is different. Art is individual. It may be of use, yet its quality transcends the use of one generation and becomes timeless.

If hard work alone were the secret of success, we would have the answer, for we know that the learned men worked hard. Many of them labored like monks in rooms so cold and damp, except close to the fires, that fingers and joints got stiff even though they swathed themselves in their thick gowns. They worked at odd hours, early in the mornings and late at night, as other duties permitted. They endured rigors that we would think beyond us.

But hard work alone, singly or in groups, does not insure a great result. Were the learned men saints, under direct inspiration?

As we have seen, these men who made the translation for King James were subject to like passions as we are. Even as they gave themselves to the great work, they yielded also to petty vanities and ambition and prejudice, and though they put into words certain counsels of perfection we have yet to attain, they behaved in their own century by a code we have outgrown. If in general we of the present day lack their piety, we do not condone their persecutions or even their fierce doctrinal hatreds. Yet we must credit them with their temporary alliance for the work in hand. Besides enduring hardships, the learned men endured each other. Their zeal for the great undertaking survived their own wrangles over doctrine and their differences of opinion in personal matters. The quarrels that are recorded were over such differences rather than the work in hand. There they must have learned to rise above themselves for the good of the whole, an act of grace deserving of reward. But does even this account for the result?

To know that the Bible words were beyond the choosing of the best of them, we have only to look at their individual writing. And this writing of theirs in books or sermons or attempted poetry also answers the suggestion that their work on the Bible was great because they lived in a great age. It was an age of great writing, in which poets and dramatists flourished, yet these men as individuals lacked the skills of those who made the Mermaid Tavern and the Globe Theater live in literature. In vain do we look to the eloquent Lancelot Andrewes or even to Miles Smith for the dulcet temper and torrents of sound in concord that mark the religious prose of Sir Thomas Browne, or for the dooming ire, like a knell, of Dr. John Donne. At the same time their Bible surpassed others in an excellence not to be attributed wholly to the original writers in the ancient tongues, so that Lytton Strachey could say of the prophets, "Isaiah and Jeremiah had the extraordinary good fortune to be translated into English by a committee of Elizabethan bishops." Badly as some of the committee could write on other occasions, not only was theirs the best of the English Bibles; there is, in no modern language, a Bible worthy to be compared with it as literature.

Though such verse as we have of their own lacks value for us, they were poets who fashioned prose without knowing how expert they were. Their meters were beyond our common attempts at scansion, but no more so than those of Donne and Blake, who are among the great English poets. Instead of rigid feet with accents, they relied on more adroit pulses, which had come to abound in their age of magic. Keats, silent on a peak as he marveled at Chapman's Homer, might have marveled still more if he had much traveled through the realms of gold in the King James Bible. Chapman's Homer of those same years no longer has the power to dazzle us, while the Bible's power has shown increase. At Oxford and Cambridge the learned men breathed the air of noble language, amid brilliant buildings and gardens which could excite them to lofty efforts, in a domain that seemed timeless. And they produced a timeless book.

Are we to say that God walked with them in their gardens? Insofar as they believed in their own calling and election, they must have believed that they would have God's help in their task. We marvel that they could both submerge themselves and assert themselves, could meekly agree yet firmly declare, and hold to the words they preferred as just and fitting. At the same time they could write and they could listen, speak clearly, and hearken to the sounds they tested, as well as to the voice of what they deemed the divine Author. And that must have been the secret of their grace and their assurance: they agreed, not with other men like themselves, but with God as their guide, and they followed not as thinking themselves righteous but as led by a righteousness beyond them. They knew that human beings are but worms, but that man when he is good and docile may mount up with wings as eagles, to be the child of God.

So they put down what they had to put down; their writing flows with a sense of *must*. Some of it they took wholly from former works, yet the *must* extends to what the 1611 scholars had the wisdom to adopt and, as it were, to inlay in the rest. A good deal of Shakespeare consists of such inlays which he made his own.

If the marvel of what they did exceeds even the marvel of Shakespeare, it is because their aim was greater, no less indeed than the salvation of their world. They were, we must remember, not writing for themselves. Their qualification for the work was that they could speak with tongues, could converse and say their prayers in the ancient languages. They were writing a Bible to help the people, for those who knew little Latin and less Greek or Hebrew. As churchmen they were in fact working against the rule of the Church, for reading Scripture would in the long run make men think for themselves and rise in protest. This John Rainolds the Puritan had seen some thirty years before he proposed a new Bible. Among six conclusions which he "propounded, expounded and defended in publick disputation" at Oxford in 1579 was a statement that "The Authoritie of the Holy Scripture is Greater Than the Authoritie of the Church." In doggerel which began with Moses and the prophets and continued through mention of the Gospels and Epistles, Rainolds concluded:

And these books hath the holy Ghost set sooth
    for mortal wightes
That we in counte of faith and light might follow
    them as lights.
Avant all ye, who braine-sicke toyes and fancies
    vain defend:
Who on humane traditions and Fathers favors depend.
The holy written Word of God doth show the perfect way
Whereby from death to life arise, from curse to
    bliss we may.

Yet if the learned men risked their churchly powers when they worked to write the vision and make it plain upon tables, that they who run might read, in return the work would raise them out of time limitations into future ages. As they went beyond time by seeking eternal right-wiseness for all, they also escaped time in the human sense; they were, as nearly as they could be, of the people of their own time, and yet they are also of our time, since they speak to us.

If now we try to define all the reasons why their work has lasted, we are sure to leave out many while giving too much weight to others. Parts of the Bible for which we have the utmost liking will seem to us apt and well-chosen without our knowing what choices the learned men had, or what the Hebrew and Greek Scriptures sought to convey. Because we have made ourselves at one with them, they confirm to us just what we ourselves think. This is true even of the odd sayings which we could never have devised, but which we have always known.

And indeed the 1611 rhythms have been potent to affect writing, speaking, and thinking ever since the learned men produced them. When Thomas Hardy suggested that the translators were made poets by the lapse of time, he overlooked this continuing influence, and certainly he cannot have read their other, unpoetic writing of the same period. The King James men not only gave us truths, and errors, which have inspired us through the ages, but had an aptness of manner with beauty as they ordered the words, and the sounds within the words, in a wondrous divine progress. They knew how to make the Bible scare the wits out of you and then calm you, all in English as superb as the Hebrew and the Greek. They could make their phrasing proceed as though caused by the First Cause, without shadow of turning; they could make the stately language of threat and wrath or the promises of tender mercy come word for word from God Himself, from the Hebrew Yahweh and from the Christian Father, Son, and Holy Ghost. "Woe unto you that desire the day of the Lord! Let judgment run down as waters, and righteousness as a mighty stream." And later they could say to us, "Be perfect, be of good comfort, be of one mind, live in peace: and the God of love and peace shall be with you." As we read we feel the divine power of judgment, and then this love and peace, this good comfort, this oneness of mind. The very word structure has the power to impress us, to arouse and quiet us, to confirm in us a basic sureness.

Soul and body, the work of the learned men still moves the world because they wrought inside each sentence a certain balance of letter and spirit. If other versions have their day and pass, it is because this balance is somehow marred, even though strict verbal accuracy may be with them. Thus to read "The grace of our Lord Jesus Christ be with you all" is for most of us a happy end, while the present-day scholar who says "The grace of our Lord Jesus Christ be with the saints" leaves us out because most of us in the present spurn sainthood as we understand the word. The work of the King James men is somehow more immediate and lively, even literally lively, as when the 1611 Bible tells us in I Peter that the redeemed shall be "lively stones."

Though we may challenge the idea of word-by-word inspiration, we surely must conclude that these were men able, in their profound moods, to transcend their human limits. In their own words, they spake as no other men spake because they were filled with the Holy Ghost. Or, in the clumsier language of our time, they so adjusted themselves to each other and to the work as to achieve a unique coordination and balance, functioning thereafter as an organic entity—no mere mechanism equal to the sum of its parts, but a whole greater than all of them.

Miles Smith in his preface bears out this idea that the work carried them above themselves. "The Scripture . . . is not an herb but a tree, or rather a whole paradise of trees of life, which bring forth fruit every month, and the fruit thereof is for meat, and the leaves for medicine . . . And what marvel? The original thereof being from heaven, not from earth; the author being God, not man; the inditer, the Holy Spirit, not the wit of the Apostles or prophets." Here we have an echo of Sir Henry Savile's distrust of wit as such, when the need is for better understanding. "But how shall men . . . understand that which is kept close in an unknown tongue? As it is written, Except I know the power of the voice,[1] I shall be to him that speaketh a barbarian, and he that speaketh shall be a barbarian to me."

"Translation it is," Smith continued, "that openeth the window, let in the light; that breaketh the shell, that we may eat the kernel; that putteth aside the curtain, that we may look into the most holy place; that removeth the cover of the well, that we may come by the water." Many other translators, such as Lancelot Andrewes, liked such figures. "While the dew lay on Gideon's fleece only, and all the earth besides was dry; then for one and the same people, which spake all of them the language of Canaan,

[1] In the King James version this is, "If I know not the meaning of the voice."

that is, Hebrew, one and the same original in Hebrew was sufficient."

Now Smith vented some modest boasting. "After the endeavors of them that were before us, we take the best pains we can in the house of God. . . . Truly (good Christian reader) we never thought from the beginning, that we should need to make a new translation, nor yet to make of a bad one a good one . . . but to make a good one better, or out of many good ones, one principal good one . . . To this purpose there were many chosen, that were greater in other men's eyes than in their own, and that sought the truth rather than their own praise . . . They trusted in him that hath the key of David, opening and no man shutting."

So, "in the confidence and with this devotion did they assemble together; not too many, lest one should trouble another; and yet many, lest many things haply might escape them. If you ask what they had before them, truly it was the Hebrew text of the old testament, the Greek of the new," which Smith compared to the two gold pipes of Revelation. They also had many Bibles in many tongues, and many books about the Bible.

The Septuagint, Smith said in passing, had reportedly taken the Greeks seventy-two days. Of the King James Bible he said, "The work hath not been huddled up in 72 days, but hath cost the workmen, as light as it seemeth, the pains of twice seven times seventy two days and more." Some who take this to mean 1,008 days ignore Smith's "and more." The work seems to have run from late 1604 through 1610, about six years.

"Neither did we disdain," Smith declared, "to revise that which we had done, and to bring back to the anvil that which we had hammered: but having and using as great helps as were needful, and fearing no reproach for slowness, nor coveting praise for expedition, we have at the length, through the good hand of the Lord upon us, brought the work to the pass that you see.

"We have not tied ourselves to an uniformity of phrasing, or to an identity of words, as some peradventure would wish that we had done. . . . For is the kingdom of God become words and syllables? . . . Niceness in words was always counted the next step to trifling." Yet we have seen the niceness with which Smith and Bilson straightened out what Bois and his comrades offered. "We desire that the Scripture may speak like itself, as in the language of Canaan, that it may be understood even of the very vulgar."

Understanding the importance of the task of translation, Smith also gave generous praise to those who had gone before. His preface contains a long passage about the translation from Hebrew into Greek, ordered by Ptolemy Philadelphus, king of Egypt: "This is the translation of the Seventy Interpreters, so called, which prepared the way for our Savior among the Gentiles by written preaching, as St. John the Baptist did among the Greeks by vocal.' Smith so well regarded this work that he thought the Seventy should be considered "not only for Interpreters but also for Prophets in some respect. . . . Yet for all that, as the Egyptians are said of the Prophets to be men and not God, and their horses flesh and not spirit, so it is evident . . . that the Seventy were Interpreters, not Prophets; they did many things well, as learned men; but yet as men they stumbled and fell, one while through oversight, another while through ignorance; yea, sometimes they might be noted to add to the original, and sometimes to take from it.'

As Smith said of the seventy, so we are still saying of the fifty-odd learned men, and again it is difficult to say where a line is to be drawn between interpretation and prophecy; for such is the communion of saints, and the

[*175*]

importance of the Word that was God. This may be the secret of our later learned men or even of the seventy before them, for as Smith describes the work: "And in what sort did these assemble? In the trust of their own knowledge, or of their sharpness of it, or deepness of judgment, as it were in an arm of flesh? At no hand. They trusted in him that hath the key of David, opening and no man shutting; they prayed to the Lord. . . ."

And so perhaps each learned man felt guided from on high, and respected, while the work lasted, one another's guiding Spirit. This we cannot know, save by the results; but Smith at least was willing to credit his predecessors in translation with some such endowment. Acknowledging as he did in his Preface a debt to the Seventy Translators of Alexandria, Miles Smith made it clear that, although he and his fellow translators for the king approached their work with fresh energy and a resolve to make new all that should be new, they were nevertheless carrying out an ancient task. However directly they might feel and acknowledge divine guidance, they were part of a human chain comparable to the "line of the prophets"—a line of interpreters maintaining the Word. Bearing its own stamp, their writing would yet be derived from and dependent on the work of others.

Chief of the sources to which they were indebted would be that translation begun by the man who prayed, from the flames at Brussels, that God would open the king of England's eyes. Tyndale had given his life for the English Bible, and had he done no more than supply the idea and make an effort at translation, he must still be accounted a pioneer of the printed Scripture. But he did more. By the royal directive which said the new Bible should be based upon the Bishops' Bible, King James actually perpetuated the work of that dangerous innovator who first planned a Bible in English print. For the Bishops' Bible traced its descent through the Matthew and the Coverdale versions straight back to Tyndale, only a Tyndale with some alterations, a royal dedication and the episcopal blessing. Disappointed in his hope to work under the patronage of the Bishop of London, driven indeed to bitter realization that not only was there "no room in my lord of London's palace to translate the New Testament, but also that there was no place to do it in all England," Tyndale the exiled heretic had obviously contributed to the translation that bishops in time approved and the king authorized to be read in churches. And now King James had commanded the use of as much of this work as should stand up under review by the learned men. Thus the martyr's prayer had an answer; a king's eyes were somewhat opened and a royal order cleared the way for the English people to have what Tyndale planned for them.

The year 1611 was too soon, perhaps, to call attention to this, but later commentators would weigh words and give Tyndale credit for much of the very phrasing of the New Testament. Word counts which estimate the debt to Tyndale in high percentages may be somewhat misleading in that the distinctive style of the King James version so depends upon the order of the words. Yet it does appear that after the best efforts of all the learned men, the final editing approved many of Tyndale's readings. Miles Smith must have known this and perhaps considered it too obvious to require comment. Indeed a criticism common to Tyndale's translation and to Smith's own style in his Preface is a certain "roughness" or crudeness which, in other estimates, is seen to be simplicity and strength. Both men liked to use the short English words. This preference for simple, familiar language may be one mark of the true interpreter.

Believing then as Christians must in the continuity of human effort, we can, while we marvel at agreement of the King James men among themselves, see them also as carrying on with understanding and sympathy the work of those who went before. The spirit of Tyndale, perhaps even of the more shadowy Wycliffe, must have been felt at Hampton Court and Stationers Hall and in the printshop under the Tiger's Head. "We are so far off from condemning any of their labors that travaileth before us in this kind, either in the land or beyond sea, either in King Henry's time, or King Edward's . . . or Queen Elizabeth's of ever renowned memory, that we acknowledge them to have been raised up of God, for the building and furnishing of his Church; and that they deserve to be had of us and of posterity in everlasting remembrance."

Such remembrance the King James men themselves have had, and have. In his introduction to a reprint of the Miles Smith preface, Edgar J. Goodspeed, himself an authority in the field of modern translation, says, "Of all the forms of the English Bible, the most distinguished and widely cherished is the King James Version," and adds that it is "predominantly the Bible of the layman, and it will undoubtedly continue to be so for a long time to come." Laymen indeed who make indiscriminate trials of the modern versions are likely to miss the familiar cadences, and to be put off by such brisk phrases as "no more delay" where eye and ear expect "time no longer." Perhaps the truth is that though we may turn to a modern translation if, unversed in ancient tongues, we want the exact meaning of a phrase, we do not feel in this reading the spiritual overtones that come through the older English words. Perhaps, when we read Scripture, we do not *want* the tempo of our own times. As an example of what a temporal translation can do, consider the work of a Dr. Harwood who in 1768 tried making the Bible over into the polite English of his era. For Matthew 14:6, "The daughter of Herodias danced before them, and pleased Herod," Dr. Harwood gave, "The daughter of Herodias, a young lady who danced with inimitable grace and elegance."

[ *178* ]

In a few centuries more, will the vision which made the King James rhythms perish from the earth? But what the people accept as vision becomes vision indeed. Granted, even the idea of God can change, has changed, and is changing. But if God today is an essence such as Alfred North Whitehead has tried to explain, it is yet clear that this Wisdom and Spirit, this basic life force, has used the King James Bible through an immense amount of living, with more to come.

When the modern translations removed the old familiar *est* and *eth* endings of verbs, they thought to make the Bible less prosy; but for many it has the opposite effect. So also to take out the "begats" seems timid and prissy, and the same is true of words deemed obscene, as in I Kings 16:11 and II Kings 18:27. The Hebrew words mean just what the King James men made them mean, what soldiers mean today. A masterpiece may use what words it pleases, and the work of the 1611 translators lasts partly because they were fearless and called a spade a spade.

But the lasting glory of the King James version is such that it is unnecessary to pick flaws in later attempts. It is our good fortune that we can have the modern versions while we keep the old Bible too. The omens are good for the work of those devout artists, the King James men, to out-weigh the more prosaic or streamlined sequents. Modern shortcomings need not deprive or embarrass us, for inepti-tudes are not new, and legions of professed poets have rendered parts of the Bible in ways so banal as to be gro-tesque. De Quincey shuddered at the thought of the Holy Scriptures as the age of Pope might have rendered them. Among the worst of poets, when he dealt with the Bible words, was John Milton. In the King James version, Psalm 1:1 reads "Blessed is the man that walketh not in the counsel of the ungodly, nor standeth in the way of sinners, nor sitteth in the seat of the scornful." Milton in 1653 made this:

> Blest is the man who hath not walked astray
> In counsel of the wicked, and in the way
> Of sinners hath not stood, and in the seat
> Of scorners hath not sat.

No wonder that the King James verse lives, while Milton's verse, for most of us, has long since died.

The author of *The Seasons* in his time had more repute as a poet than the King James men had in their time. Yet here is what James Thomson did to Matthew 6:28, 29: "And why take ye thought for raiment? Consider the lilies of the field, how they grow; they toil not, neither do they spin: and yet I say unto you, that even Solomon in all his glory was not arrayed like one of these." Now Thomson: [2]

> Observe the rising lily's snowy grace,
> Observe the various vegetable race;
> They neither toil nor spin, but careless grow;
> Yet see how warm they blush! how bright they glow!
> What regal vestments can with them compare,
> What king so shining, and what queen so fair?

We can appraise how good the 1611 Bible is by sounding such depths of badness. The King James version has endured partly because its translators had ears to hear when the morning stars sang together, and all the sons of God shouted for joy.

The learned men did misread some words and phrases. Having to denote and connote at the same time, like all other writers, they sometimes missed their marks. They had fewer tools of Biblical scholarship than we have today, and some they had were of inferior quality. Yet many have treasured as beauty what are no doubt mistakes in phrasing. Does that matter much? There were varied and faulty readings in the oldest texts; many of them still remain and always will. Though modern scholars desire to pre-

[2] *Paraphrase on the Latter Part of the Sixth Chapter of St. Matthew.*

sent a truer translation, their success is limited and relative; they can at best only approach truth.

If the strange doings, the wisdom and the advice, the maxims, the divine rages and the promised rewards of the King James version excite and bother us, no doubt the English Bible has lasted partly because it *has* bothered us, and those scholars who try to take the bother out make it too common. Like a mountain, the King James Bible gives us much to do if we are to learn much of it, and like fire in the air it plays for us with changing lights. When all is said and done, we have lived too long with the land, air, and water of 1611, with its people, their concepts and actions, to change with ease. When a true masterpiece is done, it stays done, it lives alone.

Can we then ever define just what the beauty of the King James Bible is, just what has made us love it? Millions of sermons, those that lasted hours, and the neat little ones of about fifteen minutes today, have made of the Bible, and the 1611 Bible above all, what they pleased. Millions of people have put themselves to it to explain it, sometimes with rash valor to explain away parts of it. And though it has given to millions the words of life to live by, people have got from it quips and cranks and wanton wiles as well as the deep things of God. They have found blessings in the very conflicts which it allows its readers.

Indeed, one reason the King James Bible lasts is that it gives us freedom to differ, affording us counterthoughts to rub against each other. Thus though the new translation captured readers slowly, in the long run it appealed to High Church, Low Church, and chapel alike. Though it was never merely a Puritan work, Cromwell and his fellow Roundheads pushed it forward. George Fox, Milton, Bunyan, and Defoe used it. Boswell quoted it roughly. In early Plymouth Elder William Brewster appears to have had only a Great Bible, yet soon Roger Williams, Increase Mather, Cotton Mather, the New Lights, Wesley, all made their teachings comport with the King James text. The heirs of Robert Barker went on printing as private owners of the right for a hundred years. At last it suited nearly all the Protestant sects. In the United States it has been the standby not only of "the Bible belt" but of all other regions. The Mormons took it with them to Utah. The Christian Science Church leans on it for lesson-sermons. Negro preachers love it. Untold millions could unite in their respect for the King James words when they could unite on almost nothing else.

Although Shakespeare did not quote from it, the King James version won praise from the great modern dramatist who himself loved fire and sparkle and debate upon all sides of a question. Writing of wide Bible distribution, Bernard Shaw declared:

In all these instances the Bible means the translation authorized by King James the First. . . . The translation was extraordinarily well done because to the translators what they were translating was not merely a curious collection of ancient books written by different authors in different stages of culture, but the word of God divinely revealed through His chosen and expressly inspired scribes. In this conviction they carried out their work with boundless reverence and care and achieved a beautifully artistic result. It did not seem possible to them that they could better the original texts; for who could improve on God's own style? And as they could not conceive that divine revelation could conflict with what they believed to be the truths of their religion, they did not hesitate to translate a negative by a positive where such a conflict seemed to arise, as they could hardly trust their own fallible knowledge of ancient Hebrew when it contradicted the very foundations of their faith, nor could they doubt that God would, as they prayed, take care that His message should not suffer corruption at their hands. In this state of exaltation they made a translation so magnificent that to this day the common human Britisher or citizen of the United States of North America accepts and wor-ships it as a single book by a single author, the book being the Book of Books and the author being God.

Today even the godless admire the splendors of the King James words, retaining them in their thoughts and on their lips as if they expressed truisms or slogans, or charming, sometimes comic aspects of the outworn. Thus they persist in our common language, and for words of power this may be enough; the Spirit that giveth life and the gospel, the good news that saves, each must find for himself. And so when some say that Jesus or the prophets must have meant this or that, perhaps we should presume to say in answer only that a statement means this or that to us. Read into the Bible what you wish; your gospel, or good news, may well be private. Can you rightly impose it on any other? We may enjoy the meanings that we find without thinking our meanings true for all, for thus all readers become priests unto God, and honor and keep faith with the learned men.

Let us end with a passage from a letter dealing with divinity, the study of divine truth, written by Dr. John Rainolds and apparently unpublished until now. In this of his papers the father of the 1611 Bible wrote that the Gospel of John and the Epistle to the Romans are "the sum of the New Testament; Isaiah the prophet and the Psalms of David the sum of the Old." Then he added:

Divinity, the knowledge of God, is the water of life. . . . God forbid that you should think that divinity consists of words, as a wood doth of trees. . . . True divinity cannot be learned unless we frame our hearts and minds wholly to it. . . . The knowledge of God must be learned of God. . . . We have to use two means, prayers and the reading of the holy Scriptures, prayers for ourselves to talk with God, and reading to hear God talk with us. . . . We must diligently give ourselves to reading and meditation of the holy Scriptures. . . . I pray God you may.

[183]

# The Translators

THE WESTMINSTER GROUPS:

| Old Testament | New Testament |
|---|---|
| (Genesis—Kings, inclusive) | (Romans—Jude, inclusive) |
| Lancelot Andrewes | William Barlow |
| William Bedwell | William Dakins |
| Francis Burleigh | Roger Fenton |
| Richard Clarke | Ralph Hutchinson |
| Jeffrey King | Michael Rabbett |
| John Layfield | Thomas Sanderson |
| John Overall | John Spenser |
| Hadrian Saravia | |
| Robert Tigue | |
| Richard Thomson | |

THE OXFORD GROUPS:

| Old Testament | New Testament |
|---|---|
| (Isaiah—Malachi, inclusive) | (Gospels, Acts, Apocalypse) |
| Richard Brett | George Abbot |
| Daniel Featley (born Fairclough) | John Aglionby |
| John Harding | John Harmer |
| Thomas Holland | Leonard Hutton |
| Richard Kilby | John Perin |
| John Rainolds | Thomas Ravis |
| Miles Smith | Henry Savile |
| | Giles Thomson |

| *Old Testament* | *Apocrypha* |
|---|---|

(I Chronicles—Ecclesiastes, inclusive)

| | |
|---|---|
| Roger Andrewes | John Bois |
| Andrew Bing | William Branthwaite |
| Laurence Chaderton | Andrew Downes |
| Francis Dillingham | John Duport |
| Thomas Harrison | Jeremy Radcliffe |
| Edward Lively | Samuel Ward |
| John Richardson | Robert Ward |
| Robert Spalding | |

Also Thomas Bilson, editor

These are the 48 scholars listed by the British Museum. To them should be added:

William Thorne, credentials supplied in this book.

Richard Edes, named for the Greek group at Oxford, but dying early, may be added. Also,

George Ryves, an overseer of the translation at Oxford.

William Eyre, James Montague, Arthur Lake, Nicholas Love, Ralph Ravens, and Thomas Sparke appear on other lists or are mentioned by some authorities as taking part in the work.

# Comparative Readings

GENESIS 8:11

*Coverdale.* She returned unto him about even tide, and behold, she had broken off a leaf of an olive tree and bare it in her nebb. Then Noah perceived that the waters were abated upon the earth.

*Geneva.* And the dove came to him in the evening, and lo, in her mouth was an olive leaf that she had plucked, Whereby Noah knew that the waters were abated from off the earth.

*King James.* And the dove came in to him in the evening, and, lo, in her mouth was an olive leaf plucked off; so Noah knew that the waters were abated from off the earth.

EXODUS 13:21

*Coverdale.* And the Lord went before them by day in a pillar of a cloud, to lead them the right way, and by night in a pillar of fire, that he might show the light to walk both by day and night.

*Geneva.* And the Lord went before them by day in a pillar of a cloud to lead them the way, and by night in a pillar of fire to give them light, that they might go both by day and by night.

*King James.* And the Lord went before them by day in a pillar of a cloud, to lead them the way; and by night in a pillar of fire, to give them light; to go by day and night.

LEVITICUS 11:21, 22

*Coverdale.* Yet these shall ye eat of the fowls that creep and go upon four feet; even those that have no knees above upon the legs, to hop withal upon the earth. Of these may ye eat, as there is the arbe with his kind, and the selaam with his kind, and the hargol with his kind, and the hagab with his kind.

*Geneva.* . . . Of them shall ye eat these, the grasshopper after his kind, the solcan after his kind, the hargol after his kind, and the hegab [1] after his kind.

*King James.* Yet these may ye eat of every flying creeping thing that goeth upon all four, which have legs above their feet, to leap withal upon the earth;

Even these of them ye may eat; the locust after his kind, and the bald locust after his kind, and the beetle after his kind, and the grasshopper after his kind.

*Revised Standard Version.* Yet among the winged insects that go on all fours you may eat those which have legs above their feet, with which to leap on the earth.

Of them you may eat: the locust according to its kind, the bald locust according to its kind, the cricket according to its kind, and the grasshopper according to its kind.

NUMBERS 21:8

*Coverdale.* Then said the Lord unto Moses, Make thee a brasen serpent, and set it up for a token. Whosoever is bitten, and looketh upon it, shall live.

*Geneva.* And the Lord said unto Moses, Make thee a fiery serpent, and set it up for a sign, that as many as are bitten shall look upon it and live.

*King James.* And the Lord said unto Moses, Make thee a fiery serpent, and set it upon a pole: and it shall come to pass, that every one that is bitten, when he looketh upon it, shall live.

DEUTERONOMY 24:5

*Coverdale.* When a man hath newly taken a wife, he shall not go out a warfare, neither shall he be charged withal. He shall be free in his house one year long, that he may be merry with his wife which he hath taken.

*Geneva.* When a man taketh a new wife, he shall not go a warfare, neither shall he be charged with any business, but

[1] The strange names were attempts to give in English letters the exact Hebrew terms.

shall be free at home one year, and rejoice with his wife which he hath taken.

*King James.* When a man hath taken a new wife, he shall not go out to war, neither shall he be charged with any business: but he shall be free at home one year, and shall cheer up his wife which he hath taken.

JOSHUA 6:20

*Coverdale.* Then made the people a great shout and the priests blew the trumpets (for when the people heard the noise of the trumpets, they made a great shout) and the walls fell, and the people climbed up in to the city, every man straight before him. Thus they won the city.

*Geneva.* So the people shouted when they had blown trumpets; for when the people had heard the sound of the trumpet, they shouted with a great shout and the wall fell down flat; so the people went up into the city, every man straight before him, and they took the city.

*King James.* So the people shouted when the priests blew with the trumpets: and it came to pass, when the people heard the sound of the trumpet, and the people shouted with a great shout, that the wall fell down flat, so that the people went up into the city, every man straight before him, and they took the city.

JUDGES 5:25–27

*Bishops' Bible.* He asked water and she gave him milk, she brought forth butter in a lordly dish. She put her hand to the nail, and her right hand to the smith's hammer; with the hammer smote she Sisera and smote his head, wounded him and pierced his temples. He bowed him down at her feet, he fell down, and lay still at her feet, he bowed himself and fell, and when he had sunk down, he lay there destroyed.

*King James.* He asked water, and she gave him milk: she brought forth butter in a lordly dish.

She put her hand to the nail, and her right hand to the workmen's hammer; and with the hammer she smote Sisera, she smote off his head, when she had pierced and stricken through his temples.

[ *188* ]

At her feet he bowed, he fell, he lay down. At her feet he bowed, he fell; where he bowed, there he fell down dead.

*Jewish Bible of 1917.* Water he asked, milk she gave him. In a lordly bowl she brought him curd. Her hand she put to the tent pin, and her right hand to the workmen's hammer . . . At her feet he sunk, he fell, he lay; at her feet he sunk, he fell; where he sunk, there he fell down dead.

JUDGES 15:16

*Coverdale.* And Samson said: With an old ass's cheek bone, yea even with the cheek bone of an ass have I slain a thousand men.

*Geneva.* Then Samson said, With the jaw of an ass are heaps upon heaps; with the jaw of an ass have I slain a thousand men.

*King James.* And Samson said, With the jawbone of an ass, heaps upon heaps, with the jaw of an ass have I slain a thousand men.

I KINGS 10:4, 5

*Coverdale.* When the queen of rich Arabia saw all the wisdom of Solomon and the house that he had builded, and the meats of his table, and the dwellings of his servants, and the offices of his ministers and their garments, and his butlers, and the burnt offerings which he offered in the house of the Lord, she wondered accordingly.

*Geneva.* Then the queen of Sheba saw all Solomon's wisdom, and the houses he had built,

And the meat of his table, and the sitting of his servants, and the order of his ministers, and their apparel, and his drinking vessels, and his burnt offerings that he offered in the house of the Lord, and she was greatly astonied.

*King James.* And when the queen of Sheba had seen all Solomon's wisdom, and the house that he had built,

And the meat of his table, and the sitting of his servants, and the attendance of his ministers, and their apparel, and his cupbearers, and his ascent by which he went up unto the house of the Lord; there was no more spirit in her.

*Geneva.* Thine, O Lord, is the greatness, and the power, and the glory, and the victory, and the praise: for all that is in the heaven and in the earth is thine; thine is the kingdom, O Lord, and thou art excellent as head above all.

*King James.* Thine, O Lord, is the greatness, and the power, and the glory, and the victory, and the majesty: for all that is in the heaven and in the earth is thine; thine is the kingdom, O Lord, and thou art exalted as head above all.

II CHRONICLES 20:21

*Coverdale.* . . . Appointed the singers unto the Lord, and them that gave praise in the beauty of holiness, to go before the harnessed men, and to say, O give thanks unto the Lord, for his mercy endureth for ever.

*Geneva.* . . . Praise him that is in the beautiful sanctuary . . . Praise ye the Lord, for his mercy lasteth for ever.

*King James.* . . . he appointed singers unto the Lord, and that should praise the beauty of holiness, as they went out before the army, and to say, Praise the Lord, for his mercy endureth for ever.

JOB 14:1, 2

*Coverdale.* Man that is born of a woman hath but a short time to live and is full of diverse miseries. He cometh up and falleth away like a flower . . .

*Geneva.* Man that is born of a woman is for short continuance and full of trouble. He shooteth forth as a flower, and is cut down . . .

*King James.* Man that is born of a woman is of few days, and full of trouble.

He cometh forth like a flower, and is cut down : . . .

JOB 42:5

*Coverdale.* I have given diligent ear unto thee, and now I see ye with mine eyes.

*Geneva, Bishops', and King James.* I have heard of thee by the hearing of the ear; but now mine eye seeth thee.

[ *190* ]

*Douay.* With the hearing of the ear I have heard thee, and now mine eye seeth thee.

*Revised Standard Version.*

> I had heard of thee by the hearing of the ear,
> but now mine eye sees thee.

## PSALMS 8:5

*Coverdale.* After thou haddest for a season made him lower than the angels, thou crownedst him with honor and glory.

*Geneva.* For thou hast made him a little lower than God, and crowned him with glory and worship.

*King James.* For thou hast made him a little lower than the angels, and hast crowned him with glory and honor.

## PSALM 23

*Geneva.* The Lord is my shepherd. I shall not want. He maketh me to rest in green pasture, and leadeth me by the still waters. . . . Doubtless kindness and mercy shall follow me all the days of my life, and I shall remain a long season in the house of the Lord.

*Bishops'.* God is my shepherd, therefore I can lack nothing. He will cause me to repose myself in pasture full of grass, and he will lead me unto calm waters. He will convert my soul . . . Truly felicity and mercy shall follow me all the days of my life, and I will dwell in the house of God for a long time.

*King James.* The Lord is my shepherd; I shall not want.

He maketh me to lie down in green pastures: he leadeth me beside the still waters.

He restoreth my soul . . .

Surely goodness and mercy shall follow me all the days of my life: and I will dwell in the house of the Lord for ever.

## PSALM 46:1

*Coverdale.* In our trouble and adversity, we have found that God is our refuge, our strength and help.

*Geneva.* God is our hope and strength and help in troubles, ready to be found.

*King James.* God is our refuge and strength, a very present help in trouble.

### PSALM 91:1, 2

*Geneva.* Whoso dwelleth in the secret place of the most High shall abide in the shadow of the Almighty.

I will say unto the Lord, O mine hope and my fortress; he is my God, in him will I trust.

*Bishops'.* Whosoever sitteth under the cover of the Most High, he shall abide under the shadow of the Almighty . . .

*Douay.* He that dwelleth in the aid of the most High shall abide under the protection of the God of Jacob . . .

*King James.* He that dwelleth in the secret place of the Most High shall abide under the shadow of the Almighty.

I will say of the Lord, he is my refuge and my fortress: my God; in him will I trust.

### PSALM 121:1

*Geneva.* I will lift mine eyes unto the mountains, from whence my help shall come.

*King James.* I will lift mine eyes unto the hills, from whence cometh my help.

*Jewish Bible of 1917.* I will lift up mine eyes unto the mountains. From whence shall my help come?

### PSALM 137:1, 2

*Coverdale.* By the waters of Babylon we sat down and wept, when we remembered Zion. As for our harps, we hanged them up upon the trees that are therein.

*Geneva.* By the rivers of Babel we sate, and there we wept, when we remembered Zion.

We hanged our harps upon the willows in the midst thereof.

*King James.* By the rivers of Babylon, there we sat down, yea, we wept, when we remembered Zion.

We hanged our harps upon the willows in the midst thereof.

### PSALM 139:7–11

*Coverdale.* Whither shall I go from thy spirit? Or whither shall I flee from thy presence? If I climb up in to heaven, thou art there. If I go down to hell, thou art there also. If I take the wings of the morning, and remain in the uttermost part of the sea, even there shall thy hand lead me, and thy right hand shall hold me. If I say, peradventure the darkness shall cover me, then shall my night be turned to day.

*Geneva.* Whither shall I go from thy spirit? Or whither shall I flee from thy presence?

If I ascend into heaven, thou art there; if I lie down in hell, thou art there.

Let me take the wings of the morning, and dwell in the uttermost parts of the sea;

Yet thither shall thine hand lead me, and thy right hand hold me.

If I say, yet the darkness shall hide me, even the night shall be light about me.

*Bishops'.* Whither can I go from thy spirit, or whither can I flee from thy face? If I ascend up into heaven, thou art there; if I lay me down in hell, thou art there also. If I take the wings of the morning, and go to dwell in the uttermost parts of the sea, even there also thy hand shall lead me, and thy right hand shall hold me. And if I say peradventure the darkness shall cover me; and the night shall be day for me.

*King James.* Whither shall I go from thy spirit? or whither shall I flee from thy presence?

If I ascend up into heaven, thou art there: if I make my bed in hell, behold, thou art there.

If I take the wings of the morning, and dwell in the uttermost parts of the sea;

Even there shall thy hand lead me, and thy right hand shall hold me.

If I say, Surely the darkness shall cover me; even the night shall be light about me.

SONG OF SOLOMON, 2:11-13

*Bishops'.*[2] For lo the winter is now passed, the rain is away and gone, the flowers are come up in the field, the time of the birds' singing is come, and the voice of the turtle dove is heard in our land . . .

*Geneva.* For behold, winter is passed, the rain is changed and is gone away.

[2] In the Bishops' Bible the book is called "The Ballet of Ballets of Solomon."

The flowers appear in the earth, the time of the singing of birds is come, and the voice of the turtle is heard in our land.

The fig tree hath brought forth her young figs, and the vines with their small grapes have cast a savor.

*King James.* For, lo, the winter is past, the rain is over and gone;

The flowers appear on the earth; the time of the singing of birds is come, and the voice of the turtle is heard in our land;

The fig tree putteth forth her green figs, and the vines with the tender grape give a good smell. . . .

ISAIAH 9:6

*Coverdale.* For unto us a child shall be born, and unto us a son shall be given. Upon his shoulder shall the government be, and he shall be called by his own name: The wondrous giver of counsel, the mighty God, the everlasting Father, the prince of peace.

*Bishops'.* For unto us a child is born, and unto us a son is given, upon his shoulder shall the rule be, and he is called with his own name, wonderful the giver of counsel, the mighty God, the everlasting Father, the prince of peace.

*Douay.* For a child is born to us, and a son is given to us, and the government is upon his shoulder, and his name shall be called Wonderful, Counsellor, God the mighty, the Father of the world to come, the prince of peace.

*King James.* For unto us a child is born, unto us a son is given: and the government shall be upon his shoulder: and his name shall be called Wonderful, Counsellor, The mighty God, The everlasting Father, The Prince of Peace.

ISAIAH 52:7

*Coverdale.* O how beautiful are the feet of the ambassador that bringeth the message from the mountain and proclaimeth peace, that bringeth the good tidings and preacheth health, that saith unto Zion, Thy God is the king.

*Geneva.* How beautiful upon the mountains are the feet of him that declareth and publisheth peace, declareth good tidings, and publisheth salvation, saying unto Zion, Thy God reigneth.

*Douay.* How beautiful upon the mountains are the feet of him that bringeth good tidings and that preacheth peace, of him that showeth forth good, that preacheth salvation, that saith to Zion, Thy God shall be king.

*King James.* How beautiful upon the mountains are the feet of him that bringeth good tidings, that publisheth peace; that bringeth good tidings of good, that publisheth salvation; that saith unto Zion, Thy God reigneth!

ISAIAH 60:19

*Bishops'.* The sun shall never be thy daylight, and the light of thy moon shall never shine unto thee; but the Lord shall be thine everlasting light; and thy God shall be thy glory.

*King James.* The sun shall be no more thy light by day; neither for brightness shall the moon give light unto thee: but the Lord shall be unto thee an everlasting light, and thy God thy glory.

ISAIAH 65:24

*Coverdale and Bishops'.* And it shall be that or ever they call, I will answer them, and while they are but thinking how to speak, I will hear them.

*King James.* And it shall come to pass, that before they call, I will answer; and while they are yet speaking, I will hear.

JOEL 3:14

*Coverdale.* In the valley appointed there shall be many, many people, for the day of the Lord is nigh in the valley appointed.

*Geneva.* O Multitude, O Multitude, come into the valley of threshing, for the day of the Lord is near in the valley of threshing.

*Bishops'.* O people, people, come into the valley of final judgment, for the day of the Lord is at hand in the valley of final judgment.

*Douay.* Nations, nations, in the valley of destruction, for the day of the Lord is near in the valley of destruction.

*King James.* Multitudes, multitudes in the valley of decision: for the day of the Lord is near in the valley of decision.

*Geneva.* He hath showed thee, O man, what is good, and what the Lord requireth of thee; firstly to do justly, and to have mercy, and to humble thy self to walk with thy God.

*King James.* He hath showed thee, O man, what is good; and what doth the Lord require of thee, but to do justly, and to love mercy, and to walk humbly with thy God?

### ZEPHANIAH 3:17

*Geneva.* The Lord thy God in the midst of thee is mighty; he will save, he will rejoice over thee with joy; he will quiet himself in his love; he will rejoice over thee with joy.

*King James.* The Lord thy God in the midst of thee is mighty; he will save, he will rejoice over thee with joy; he will rest in his love, he will joy over thee with singing.

### ZECHARIAH 14:20

*Geneva.* In that day shall there be written upon the bridles of horses, The holiness unto the Lord.

*King James.* In that day shall there be upon the bells of the horses, Holiness unto the Lord. . . .

### MALACHI 4:2

*Coverdale.* . . . Ye shall go forth and multiply as the fat calves.

*Geneva.* But unto you that fear my name shall the sun of righteousness arise, and health shall be under his wings, and ye shall go forth and grow up as fat calves.

*Bishops'.* But to you that fear my name shall that son of righteousness arise, and health shall be under his wings, and ye shall go forth and skip like fat calves.

*King James.* But unto you that fear my name shall the Sun of righteousness arise with healing in his wings, and ye shall go forth, and grow up as calves of the stall.

### MATTHEW 5:13

*Tyndale.* If the salt have lost his saltness, what can be salted therewith?

*King James.* If the salt have lost his savor, wherewith shall it be salted?

*Tyndale.* When ye pray, babble not much, as the heathen do, for they think that they shall be heard for their much babblings sake.

*King James.* But when ye pray, use not vain repetitions, as the heathen do: for they think that they shall be heard for their much speaking.

MATTHEW 6:10

*Bishops'.* Let thy kingdom come, Thy will be done, as well in earth as it is in heaven.

*King James.* Thy kingdom come. Thy will be done in earth, as it is in heaven.

MATTHEW 6:33

*Tyndale.* Seek ye first the kingdom of heaven and the righteousness thereof.

*King James.* But seek ye first the kingdom of God, and his righteousness . . .

MATTHEW 10:9

*Tyndale.* Possess not gold, nor silver, nor brass in your girdles.

*King James.* Provide neither gold, nor silver, nor brass in your purses.

LUKE 2:14

*Coverdale.* Glory be unto God on high, and peace upon earth, and unto men a good will.

*Geneva.* Glory be to God in the high heavens, and peace in earth, and towards men good will.

*Bishops'.* Glory to God in the highest and peace on the earth, and among men a good will.

*Douay.* Glory to God in the highest, and on earth peace to men of good will.

*King James.* Glory to God in the highest, and on earth peace, good will toward men.

LUKE 6:32

*Tyndale.* . . . for the very sinners love their lovers.

*King James.* . . . for sinners also love those that love them.

*Coverdale*. The eye is the light of the body.

*Geneva*. The light of the body is the eye.

*Bishops'*. The candle of the body is the eye.

*Douay*. The light of the body is the eye. If thy eye be single, thy whole body will be lightsome; but if it be evil thy body also will be darksome.

*King James*. The light of the body is the eye; therefore when thine eye is single, thy whole body also is full of light; but when thine eye is evil, thy body also is full of darkness.

### LUKE 22:56

*Tyndale*. And one of the wenches beheld him as he sat by the fire and set good eyesight on him.

*King James*. But a certain maid beheld him as he sat by the fire, and earnestly looked upon him . . .

### JOHN 14:2

*Coverdale*. In my Father's house are many dwellings.

*Geneva and Bishops'*. In my Father's house are many dwelling places.

*Douay*. In my Father's house there are many mansions.

*King James*. In my Father's house are many mansions.

*Revised Standard Version*. In my Father's house are many rooms.

### JOHN 14:27

*Tyndale*. . . . Let not your heart be grieved, neither fear ye.

*King James*. . . . Let not your heart be troubled, neither let it be afraid.

### JOHN 15:12

*Tyndale*. . . . That ye love together . . .

*King James*. . . . That ye love one another . . .

### JOHN 15:13

*Tyndale*. Greater love than this hath no man, than that a man bestow his life for his friends.

*Coverdale.* No man hath greater love than to set his life for his friend.

*Bishops'.* Greater love than this hath no man, when any man bestoweth his life for his friends.

*King James.* Greater love hath no man than this, that a man lay down his life for his friends.

I CORINTHIANS 13:4

*Bishops'.* Charity suffereth long and is courteous, charity envieth not, charity doth not frowardly, swelleth not.

*King James.* Charity suffereth long, and is kind; charity envieth not; charity vaunteth not itself, is not puffed up.

II CORINTHIANS 1:5

*Tyndale.* For as the afflictions of Christ are plenteous in us, even so is our consolation plenteous by Christ.

*King James.* For as the sufferings of Christ abound in us, so our consolation also aboundeth by Christ.

II CORINTHIANS 3:18

*Geneva.* But we all behold as in a mirror the glory of the Lord with open face, and are changed into the same image from glory to glory as by the spirit of the Lord.

*King James.* But we all, with open face beholding as in a glass the glory of the Lord, are changed into the same image from glory to glory, even as by the Spirit of the Lord.

II CORINTHIANS 4:1, 2

*Tyndale.* Therefore seeing that we have such an office, even as mercy is come on us, we faint not; but have cast from us the cloaks of unhonesty, and walk not in craftiness, neither corrupt we the word of God; but walk in the truth, and report ourselves to every man's conscience in the sight of God.

*King James.* Therefore seeing we have this ministry, as we have received mercy, we faint not;

But have renounced the hidden things of dishonesty, not walking in craftiness, nor handling the word of God deceitfully; but by manifestation of the truth commending ourselves to every man's conscience in the sight of God.

*Bishops'.* And sware by him that liveth for ever and ever, who created heaven, and the things that therein are, and the earth, and the things that therein are, and the sea, and the things which are therein, that there should be no longer time.

*King James.* And sware by him that liveth for ever and ever, who created heaven, and the things that therein are, and the earth, and the things that therein are, and the sea, and the things which are therein, that there should be time no longer.

*Revised Standard Version.* And swore by him who lives for ever and ever, who created heaven, and what is in it, the earth and what is in it, and the sea and what is in it, that there should be no more delay.

### REVELATION 21:2

*Geneva.* And I John saw the holy city New Jerusalem come down from God out of heaven prepared as a bride trimmed for her husband.

*Bishops'.* And I John saw the holy city, New Jerusalem, come down from God out of heaven, prepared as a bride garnished for her husband.

*King James.* And I John saw the holy city, new Jerusalem, coming down from God out of heaven, prepared as a bride adorned for her husband.

### REVELATION 21:4

*Tyndale.* . . . for the old things are gone.
*King James.* . . . for the former things are passed away.

### REVELATION 22:17

*Tyndale, Bishops' and King James.* And the Spirit and the bride say, Come. And let him that heareth say, Come. And let him that is athirst come. And whosoever will, let him take the water of life freely.

*Revised Standard Version.* The Spirit and the Bride say, "Come." And let him who hears say, "Come." And let him who is thirsty come, let him who desires take the water of life without price.

# Bibliography

### THE TRANSLATORS, THEIR WRITING

Abbot, George. *A Brief Description of the Whole World*. London, 1656.

——. *An Exposition Upon the Prophet Jonah*. London, 1613.

——. *The Reasons Which Dr. Hill Hath Brought for the Upholding of Papistry*. Oxford, 1604.

Andrewes, Lancelot. *Works*. 11 vols. Oxford, 1854.

Barlow, William. *The Sum and Substance of the Conference*. London, 1638.

——. *An Answer to a Catholic English Man*. London, 1609.

——. *A Defense of the Articles of the Protestants' Religion*. London, 1601.

——. *Sermons*. 1606, 1607.

Bedwell, William. *The Arabian Trudgman*. London, 1615.

——. *Description of Tottenham High Cross*. London, 1617.

Bilson, Thomas. *Sermons*. London, 1599–1610.

Chaderton, Laurence. *Sermons*. 1580, 1584.

Clarke, Richard. *Sermons*. London, 1637.

Dillingham, Francis. *A Golden Key, Opening the Locke to Eternal Happiness*. London, 1609.

Fenton, Roger. *An Answer to William Alabaster*. London, 1599.

——. *Of Sinning and Sacrifice*. London, 1604.

——. *A Treatise on Usury*. London, 1611.

Holland, Thomas. *Sermons*. Oxford, 1599, 1601.

Hutton, Lionel. *An Answer to a Certain Treatise of the Cross in Baptism*. Oxford, 1605.

Kilby, Richard. *The Burden of a Loaded Conscience*. Cambridge, 1608.

Layfield, John. "A Large Relation of the Porto Rico Voyage." In Samuel Purchas: *Hakluytus Posthumus, or Purchas His Pilgrims,* vol. 16. Glasgow, 1906.

Lively, Edward. *A True Chronology of the Times of the Persian Monarchy.* London, 1597.

Overall, John. *Bishop Overall's Convocation Book.* Oxford, 1690.

Rainolds, John. *The Overthrow of Stage Plays.* 1599.

———. *The Prophecy of Obadiah Opened and Applied.* Oxford, 1636.

———. *Sermon 10 on Haggai.* 1599.

———. *The Sum of the Conference Between John Rainolds and John Hart.* London, 1585.

Saravia, Hadrian. *Defensi Tractiones.* London, 1610.

———. *Diversi Tractatus.* London, 1611.

———. *Examen Tractatus.* London, 1611.

———. *A Treatise on the Different Degrees of the Christian Priesthood.* Oxford, 1590.

Savile, Henry. *The End of Nero.* London, 1591.

———. *Johannes St. Chrysostomus.* Opera Graeca. 8 vols. London, 1613.

Smith, Miles. *Sermons.* London, 1632.

Spenser, John. *God's Love to His Vineyard.* London, 1615.

Thomson, Richard. *Diatriba.* Leyden, 1616.

———. *Elenchus Refutationis.* London, 1611.

Thorne, William. *A Kenning Glass for a Christian King.* London, 1603.

Ward, Samuel. Diary in *Two Elizabethan Puritan Diaries,* ed. by M. M. Knappen. London, 1933.

### BIOGRAPHIES

Aubrey, John. *Brief Lives.* London, 1949.

Brook, Benjamin. *The Lives of the Puritans.* 3 vols. London, 1813.

Cecil, Algernon. *A Life of Robert Cecil.* London, 1915.

Colville, Kenneth N. *Fame's Twilight.* Boston, 1824.

Creasy, Edward. *Memoirs of Eminent Etonians.* London, 1876.

*Dictionary of National Biography,* London.

Dillingham, William. *Vita Chadertoni*. London, 1700. Trans. by E. S. Schuckburgh. London, 1884.

Eliot, T. S. *For Lancelot Andrewes*. London, 1928.

Fuller, Thomas. *The History of the Worthies of England*. 3 vols. London, 1840.

Hook, Walter F. *An Ecclesiastical Biography*. 8 vols. London, 1845–52.

———. *Lives of the Archbishops of Canterbury*. London, 1875.

Isaacson, Henry. *An Exact Narrative of the Life and Death of the Late Reverend and Learned Prelate and Painful Divine, Lancelot Andrewes*. London, 1650.

Neal, Daniel. *History of the Puritans*. London, 1822.

Newcourt, Richard. *Repertorium Ecclesiasticum*. 2 vols. London, 1708–10.

Ottley, Robert L. *Lancelot Andrewes*. London, 1894.

Peile, John. *Biographical Register of Christ's College*. Cambridge, 1910.

Russell, Arthur T. *Memoirs of . . . Lancelot Andrewes*. London, 1863.

Smith, Thomas. *Select Memoirs of the Lives, Labors and Sufferings of Those Pious and Learned English and Scottish Divines*. Glasgow, 1821.

Teale, William H. *Lives of English Divines*. London, 1846.

Walker, Anthony. "Life and Death of the Rev. John Bois." In Peck, Francis, *Desiderata Curiosa*. London, 1779.

Williamson, George C. *George, Third Earl of Cumberland . . . His Life and His Voyages*. Cambridge, 1920.

Winwood, Ralph. *Memorials of Affairs of State*, vol. 2. London, 1723.

Wordsworth, Christopher. *Ecclesiastical Biography*, vol. 4. London, 1810.

### THE TIME AND THE PLACE

Aydelotte, Frank. *Elizabethan Rogues and Vagabonds*. Oxford, 1913.

Burnet, Gilbert. *The History of the Reformation of the Church of England*. London, 1679–1715.

Calderwood, David. *The History of the Kirk of Scotland*. 8 vols. Edinburgh, 1842–49.

Cardwell, Edward. *A History of Conferences*. Oxford, 1841.

Chamberlain, John. *Letters*. 2 vols. Philadelphia, 1939.

Collier, Jeremy. *Ecclesiastical History of Great Britain*. 2 vols. London, 1708.

Dekker, Thomas. *The Gull's Hornbook*. London, 1609.

Disraeli, Isaac. *Miscellanies of Literature*, vol. 3. New York, 1841.

Duncan, Jonathan. *The History of Guernsey*. London, 1841.

Fuller, Thomas. *Abel Redivivus*. 2 vols. London, 1867.

———. *The Church History of Britain*. 6 vols. Oxford, 1845.

Kington, Alfred. *A History of Royston*. Royston, 1906.

Kittredge, George L. *Witchcraft in Old and New England*. Cambridge, Mass., 1929.

Law, Ernest. *A Short History of Hampton Court*. London, 1924.

Lindsay, Philip. *Hampton Court, A History*. London, 1948.

Mitman, Henry H. *Annals of St. Paul's Cathedral*. London, 1869.

Neale, John P. *The History of Antiquities of the Abbey Church of St. Peter, Westminster*. 2 vols. London, 1818.

Paquot, Jean Noel. *Histoire Littéraire des Pays-Bas*. 1763.

Pigot, Hugh. *Hadleigh*, vol. 3. Suffolk Institute of Archeology, Statistics and Natural History. Lowestoft, 1863.

Prynne, William. *Canterbury's Doom*. London, 1646.

Siltzer, Frank. *Newmarket*. London, 1923.

Sinclair, William M. *Memorials of St. Paul's Cathedral*. London, 1909.

Strype, John. *The Life and Acts of John Whitgift*. Oxford, 1822.

Willis, Browne. *A Survey of the Cathedrals*. 3 vols. London, 1742.

THE KING

Birch, Thomas. *The Court and Times of James I*. London, 1848.

Chambers, Robert. *Life of King James I*. Edinburgh, 1830.

Goodman, Godfrey. *The Court of King James the First*. 2 vols. London, 1839.

Henderson, T. F. *James I and James VI*. Edinburgh, 1904.

James I, King. *Works.* Trans. James Montagu, 1616. Including
"The Essaye of a Prentice in the Divine Art of Poesie."

Nichols, John. *The Progresses, Processions and Magnificent
Festivities of King James the First.* London, 1828.

### THE COLLEGES

Boas, Frederick S. *University Drama in the Tudor Age.* Oxford,
1914.

Chalmers, Alexander. *A History of the University of Oxford.*
2 vols. Oxford, 1810.

Clark, Andrew. *The Colleges of Oxford.* London, 1892.

Coombe, William. *A History of the University of Cambridge.*
2 vols. London, 1815.

Cooper, Charles Henry. *Athenae Cantabrigiensis.* 3 vols. Cambridge, 1861.

Fowler, Thomas. *The History of Corpus Christi College.* Oxford, 1893.

Fuller, Thomas. *The History of the University of Cambridge.*
London, 1840.

Gray, Arthur. *Cambridge University.* Cambridge, 1926.

Macray, William D. *Annals of the Bodleian Library.* London,
1868.

Mullinger, James Bass. *The University of Cambridge.* Cambridge, 1884.

Phelps, William Lyon. *George Chapman.* New York, 1895.

Ringler, William. *The Immediate Sources of Euphuism.* Modern Language Association, vol. 53. September, 1938.

Shuckburgh, Evelyn S. *Emmanuel College.* London, 1904.

Thompson, Henry L. *Christ Church.* London, 1900.

Wood, Anthony. *Athenae Oxoniensis.* London, 1815.

Young, Karl. *William Gager's Defense of the Academic Stage.*
Wisconsin Academy of Sciences, Arts and Letters, vol. 18,
part 2, 1916.

### THE GREAT WORK

Anderson, Christopher. *Annals of the English Bible.* London,
1862.

Arber, Edward. *A Transcript of the Registers of the Company
of Stationers.* London, 1877.

Ball, William. *A Brief Treatise Concerning the Regulation of Printing*. London, 1651.

Butterworth, C. C. *The Literary Lineage of the English Bible*. Philadelphia, 1951.

Eadie, John. *The English Bible*, vol. 2. London, 1876.

Heaton, W. J. *The Puritan Bible*. London, 1913.

Lewis, John. *A Complete History of the Several Translations of the Holy Bible*. London, 1918.

McClure, Alexander W. *The Translators Revived*. New York, 1853.

Penniman, Josiah H. *A Book About the English Bible*. New York, 1919.

Pollard, Alfred W. *Records of the Bible*. Oxford, 1911.

Selden, John. *Table Talk*. London, 1689.

Westcott, Brooke F. *A General View of the History of the English Bible*. New York, 1868.

Willoughby, Edwin Elliott. *The Making of the King James Bible*. Los Angeles, 1956.

### MANUSCRIPTS

Bodleian Library, Oxford. "Notes by John Bois." "Will and correspondence of John Rainolds." "Reg. XXXII 48. History of five years of the reign of James I."

Cambridge University Library. "Letters of Bishop Bancroft, 1604."

Lambeth Palace Library, London. Letter to Laurence Chaderton, June 26, 1599. Early list of translators.

Public Record Office, London. Jan. 12, 1604. Appointments for the Hampton Court conference. July 22, 1604. Translators to be chosen. April 29, 1605. Promotion for Dr. Layfield. 1606. Certificate signed by bishops, promotion of Dr. Thorne, translator. Correspondence about election of Bishop Ravis. Reports of beheading of Earl of Essex. Letter of Cecil to Dr. Barlow. Letters of Sir Henry Savile.

Yale University Library, New Haven. Typescript, "John Overall," by Nadine Overall.

# Index

Tower of London, 10, 23, 105, 108, 153
"Treacle" Bible, 10
Trinity College, 14, 30, 35, 40, 60, 99
Tyndale, William, 8, 9, 11, 27, 71, 126, 176-178

Unitarians, 142
United States, 182
University College, 53, 55, 81, 99
Ussher, James, 103
Utah, 182

Verb endings, 179
Vere, Lady Susan, 78
Victoria, Queen, 151
Villiers, George, 154, 162
Virginia, 97, 100, 105
Vulgate, 7, 9, 77

WPA, 167
Walker, Anthony, 112
Walloon Confession, 34
Walsingham, Sir Francis, 16, 18, 23, 28, 134
Walton, Isaac, 35

Ward, Robert, 61, 111
Ward, Samuel, 61, 62, 69, 111, 141, 165, 166
Wesley, John, 182
West Indies, 35, 156
Westminster, 13, 14, 16, 19, 30, 32, 34, 35, 39, 41, 42, 72, 90, 98, 102, 103, 110, 112, 115, 123
Westminster groups, 30-45, 68
Westminster Abbey, 149, 151, 161
Whitehead, Alfred North, 179
Whitgift, John, 3, 5, 12, 13, 18, 20, 42, 51, 65, 143, 158
Whitchurch Bible, 71
Whitehall, 12, 78, 79, 87, 90, 104, 107, 137, 142
Whittaker, Dr., 60
Whittingham, William, 9
Windsor, 152
Witchcraft, 54, 104-105
Wolsey, Cardinal, 1, 50
Worthington, Dr. Thomas, 128
Wotton, Sir Henry, 46
Wycliffe, 7, 178

Zouache, Edward, 157
Zwingli, 9

# COLLEGE LIBRARY

## Date Due

| Due | Returned | Due | Returned |
|-----|----------|-----|----------|
| MAY 3 0 1991 | APR 3 0 1991 | | |
| | | | |
| | | | |
| | | | |
| | | | |
| | | | |
| | | | |
| | | | |
| | | | |
| | | | |
| | | | |
| | | | |
| | | | |
| | | | |
| | | | |
| | | | |
| | | | |
| | | | |
| | | | |
| | | | |
| | | | |
| | | | |
| | | | |
| | | | |
| | | | |
| | | | |
| | | | |
| | | | |
| | | | |
| | | | |

CPSIA information can be obtained
at www.ICGtesting.com
Printed in the USA
BVOW09s0753090517

483603BV00012B/121/P